D0729664

Terry Johnson
Plays: 1

Insignificance, Unsuitable for Adults,
Cries from the Mammal House

Insignificance: 'At first glance, it looks like a game of Theatrical Consequences. What if four icons of Ike's America – Marilyn Monroe, Albert Einstein, Joe DiMaggio and Senator McCarthy – met in a NewYork hotel room in 1953? . . . A piece that works on just about every level: the intellectual, the emotional, the playful . . . one of the landmark plays of the decade.' *Guardian*
'Compassionate, witty and intelligent.' *Daily Telegraph*

Unsuitable for Adults: 'Set in the world of pub entertainment in Paddington – lunchtimes of striptease, evenings of the more violent kind of comic routine . . . it's a very funny play and very clever.' *Sunday Times*
'Johnson's script, funny and horrifying by turns, and maturely refusing to assume anything about its characters, is as fine and enduring a depiction of the current state of play in the world of love, sex, and comedy as anything ever seen on the London stage.' *Time Out*

Cries from the Mammal House: 'Set in a small English private zoo and also in the bowels of anyone who has ever had to take responsibility for others . . . Freewheeling, tough, lyrical and thrillingly unpredictable.' *Sunday Times*
'Glittering like a ball of mercury as it darts erratically hither and thither.' *Daily Telegraph*

Terry Johnson's plays include *Amabel* (Bush, London, 1979); *Days Here So Dark* (Paines Plough at the Tricycle, London, 1981); *Insignificance* (Royal Court, London, 1982 and filmed by Nicholas Roeg, 1985); *Cries from the Mammal House* (Open Heart Enterprises with the Royal Court, London, 1984); *Unsuitable for Adults* (Bush, London, 1984); *Tuesday's Child*, written with Kate Lock (Theatre Royal, Stratford East, 1985); *Imagine Drowning* (Hampstead Theatre, London, 1991 and three-part adaptation for BBC TV, 1991); *Hysteria* (Royal Court, London, 1993; Duke of York's Theatre as part of the Royal Court Classics season, 1995); *Dead Funny* (Hampstead Theatre, London, 1994).

by the same author

Hysteria
Imagine Drowning
Dead Funny

TERRY JOHNSON

Plays: 1

Insignificance
Unsuitable for Adults
Cries from the Mammal House

with an introduction by Rob Ritchie

Methuen Drama

Published by Methuen Drama in 2005

Methuen Drama
A&C Black Publisher's Limited
36 Soho Square W1D 3QY

www.methuendrama.com

5 7 9 10 8 6 4

Insignificance was first published in 1983
Copyright © 1982, 1993 by Terry Johnson

Unsuitable for Adults was first published by Faber and Faber Ltd in 1985
Copyright © 1985, 1993 by Terry Johnson

Cries from the Mammal House was first published in 1984
Copyright © 1984, 1993 by Terry Johnson

This collection copyright © Methuen Publishing Ltd 1993, 2005
Introduction copyright © 1993 by Rob Ritchie

The author has asserted his moral rights under the Copyright, Designs
and Patents Act, 1988, to be identified as the author of this work

A CIP catalogue record for this book is available from the British Library

ISBN: 978-0-413-68200-0

Typeset by SX Composing DTP, Rayleigh, Essex

Caution
All rights in this play are strictly reserved.
Application for performance, etc., should be made before rehearsals begin
to The Agency, 24 Pottery Lane, Holland Park, London W11 4LZ.
No performance may be given unless a licence has been obtained.

This book is sold subject to the condition that it shall not, by way of
trade or otherwise, be lent, resold, hired out, or otherwise circulated in
any form of binding or cover other than that in which it is published and
without a similar condition, including this condition, being imposed on
the subsequent purchaser.

Contents

Chronology

1979   *Amabel* Bush Theatre

1981   *Days Here So Dark* Paines Plough

1982   *Insignificance* Royal Court Theatre. SWET nominations for Best Play and Best Newcomer. Plays and Players Award, Evening Standard Award (Most Promising Playwright). Performed US, Germany, France, Australia, Israel, New Zealand, Japan

1983   *Bellevue* Welfare State International

1984   *Cries From The Mammal House* Royal Court/ Leicester Haymarket

1984   *Unsuitable For Adults* Bush Theatre. Performed in US, New Zealand, Australia, Canada

1985   *Tuesday's Child* BBC TV. Co-written with Kate Lock

1985   *Time Trouble* BBC TV

1985   *Insignificance* Screenplay for Recorded Picture Co.

1986   *Tuesday's Child* Theatre Royal, Stratford East. Co-written with Kate Lock

1991   *Imagine Drowning* Hampstead Theatre. Winner of the John Whiting Award, 1991

1993   *Hysteria* Royal Court Theatre. Winner of the Olivier Award for Best Comedy 1993, and Writers' Guild Award for Best West End Play

1993   *99 to 1* Carlton TV

1994   *Dead Funny* Hampstead, Vaudeville and Savoy Theatres. Winner of Critics' Circle Award for Best New Play, Writers' Guild Award for Best West End Play, 1994 Time Out Drama Award

Introduction

I first read *Insignificance*, the earliest of the plays in this collection, in the spring of 1981. At the time, I was literary manager at the Royal Court and Terry Johnson, as far as I knew, was the author of a modestly successful play about a famous painter with short legs. *Amabel*, the play in question, had wit, energy and the *sine qua non* of any show featuring Toulouse-Lautrec, a bearded actor shuffling about on his knees. It also had, or so it seemed to me, a cheerful disregard for the pressing issues of the day. Thatcher, police corruption, the Yorkshire Ripper, Poland, these were the current obsessions at the Court. Stunted French artists just didn't come into it. Given what I'd heard about Terry – there were rumours of a retreat to a Scottish island and an enthusiasm for the zanier exploits of Ken Campbell – I saw no immediate reason to try and tempt him with a commission for the Court. Apart from anything else, another company – Paines Plough – had already beaten me to it.

And then, out of the blue, *Insignificance* arrived. It wasn't my first encounter with Einstein as a fictional character. Renewed anxiety about nuclear weapons triggered several plays in the early 80s that dusted down old-fashioned biographies of the great man or dispatched him to some blasted terrain to mumble apologies to crazed mutants. *Insignificance* had none of the earnest posturing of these plays. It wasn't even about the bomb. It was a fantasy, a pure flight of imagination that brought Einstein and Marilyn Monroe, the models for the Professor and the Actress, to a New York hotel room for an unexpected exchange of views. This was such a striking conceit – Marilyn Monroe demonstrating the General Theory of Relativity – that I didn't immediately grasp how skilfully it served the underlying purpose of the play. What was obvious at once was the cool assurance of the writing. Fast, funny and elegantly structured, *Insignificance* was a true original. It was clear we had to produce it.

A year or so later, we did. Exactly why it took so long I no longer recall. There was some debate about whether the piece was best suited to the Theatre Upstairs or the main stage. And the Falklands war doubtless stirred feelings that a tough, no-nonsense report on the state of the nation ought to take precedence over a stylish comedy about the state of the universe. But, in the end, the play was simply too good to miss. Les Waters, an early champion, directed the show on the main stage and Judy Davis, much in vogue following her success in the film *My Brilliant Career*, paid her own air fare from Australia to take on the Actress. By a strange coincidence, wholly appropriate to a piece that makes memorable play with the laws of probability, the director and two of the cast had already had an unwitting hand in *Insignificance*. As originally conceived, the play featured Einstein, Monroe and the reclusive tycoon Howard Hughes. Midway through the first draft, however, Terry made an impromptu visit to the Theatre Upstairs to see what Sam Shepard's *Seduced* was about. It was about Howard Hughes – exit Terry Johnson in a cold sweat – it's a long stagger down from the Theatre Upstairs. Exit Howard Hughes to make way for Senator Joe McCarthy. That Les Waters, Larry Lamb and Ian McDiarmid, the director and cast of *Seduced*, should rematerialise eighteen months later to bring *Insignificance* to life is one of the great coincidences of our time. I like to think this restored Terry's faith in the universe.

Had *Insignificance* begun life as a feature film – Nicolas Roeg directed the screen version some years later – it's a safe bet success would have brought endless invitations to repeat the recipe. Jayne Mansfield and Max Plank in a sauna, Julie Andrews and Wittgenstein go shopping. Reading the play alongside *Unsuitable for Adults* and *Cries from the Mammal House* is a reminder that theatre in the 80s still allowed writers the freedom to be different.

This wasn't always appreciated at the time. It was often said – Michael Billington said it the week *Insignificance* went into rehearsal – that playwrights took on too many commissions, working up ideas to order rather than waiting for more elevated inspiration. Faced with endless crises of cash and confidence, managements doubtless made exaggerated claims about the wealth of talent on the books and rushed on work to prove the point. But in the years before yuppies and mobile phones came to define the achievements of Thatcher's England, the pressure on writers was never too much work. The early 80s were grim, recessive times. The real pressure was how to make sense of what was happening.

Unsuitable for Adults captures the mood exactly. A murderous rapist stalking the streets, a grotty pub venue where nothing works. The play has many incidental pleasures – a restless curiosity about character, brisk comic dialogue – but it's the sense of trapped energies and broken hopes that endures. At first sight, the assembled talents have little obvious connection with the legendary stars of *Insignificance*. Stripper Trish may be pretty and highly strung but she is plainly no Marilyn Monroe. Yet she and comedian Kate share a common problem with the American film star. All three women are trapped, locked in bruising relationships with men. Sex, glamour, availability are the roles on offer and there's no easy escape to a fuller identity. If the Actress proves she is no dumb blonde she nevertheless leaves the play to resume her performance as the ultimate male fantasy while Kate is reduced to a desperate act of self-mutilation as she struggles to break free.

This sounds depressing. The opening image of *Cries from the Mammal House* – the slow slaughter of the animals – is certainly no less bleak. But these plays are comedies. When Kate and Trish escape to Dartmoor, it is to discover a renewed sense of possibility. The tiny celebration of the power of the imagination that forms the epilogue to the play is an impulse given free rein in *Mammal House*, the most obviously experimental of the plays. The dreamlike second act is a wonderful piece of invention and it produces my favourite stage direction: 'He goes, deep in Western thought.' But if there is one image that fixes the characteristic optimism of Terry's work, it is surely the miraculous survival of the dodo. It is a moment of pure theatre that sends you out into the night feeling better for having made the journey. Ten years later, it's a pleasure to recall the experience.

Rob Ritchie
August 1993

Insignificance

For Kenneth Hardacre

I believe with Schopenhauer that one of the strongest
motives that leads men to Art and Science is escape
from everyday life with its painful crudity and hopeless
dreariness, from the fetters of one's ever-shifting
desires. With this negative motive there goes a positive
one. Man tries to make for himself in the fashion that
suits him best a simplified and intelligible picture of this
world: he then tries to some extent to substitute this
cosmos of his for the world of experience and thus to
overcome it. Each makes this cosmos and its
construction the pivot of his emotional life in order to
find in this way the peace and security he cannot
find . . .

Albert Einstein

Insignificance was first performed at the Royal Court Theatre, London, on 8 July 1982, with the following cast:

Professor	Ian McDiarmid
Senator	William Hootkins
Actress	Judy Davis
Ballplayer	Larry Lamb
Heavy	

Directed by Les Waters
Designed by Tony McDonald

Characters

The Professor   *White haired and bright eyed. Around seventy years old. He wears a shabby sweatshirt and a loose dark suit. He thinks a great deal and speaks concisely.*

The Senator   *A fat, red, sweaty man wearing a large, pale, sweaty suit.*

The Actress   *A stunning blonde carefully composed to look a little younger than she is. Listening to her one might guess at twenty years, or at other times forty.*

The Ballplayer   *All-American boy turned forty. He resembles a retired astronaut.*

The Heavy   *Tall, dark mobster type, probably CIA.*

Setting

1953. A hotel room. New York.

The room is modern, circa '53, and has a large expanse of window looking out on to the city. There are stars and there is light from a neon sign on a building below. There is a door to the corridor, one to the bathroom, and a double bed.

Act One

A New York hotel room, 1953, night.

The **Professor** *sits with a pad, calculating.*

He is seventy, white haired, bright eyed. He wears a shabby Princeton sweatshirt and has bare feet. Beside him is a pile of paper a foot tall. A Gladstone bag lies on the bed, a clock is ticking.

He hears a cheer in the distance and goes to the open window. His face is lit by flashing red neon. He looks upward.

There is a knock on the door.

Senator (*offstage*) Professor?

The **Professor** *goes to the door.*

The **Senator** *stands with a bottle, like a nightmare salesman. He is a fat, sweaty man in a pale sweaty suit.*

Senator It's a dog of a night, Professor. I got bourbon or I got rye. Sort of a peace offering for calling on you so late but I couldn't see as how you'd be sleeping on a night like this. You'll have to forgive my intrusion but I've got something to say to you that's just got to be said before the morning. This is a hell of a hotel, ain't it? You have a good flight? Each time I fly there is half as much time spent in the air and twice as much spent in the terminal. Progress. Yes sir. Now we got whisky, we got glasses, and we got the whole night ahead of us. Half the night for you and half the night for me.

Professor Thank you no, I don't drink.

Senator And I don't take no for an answer, Professor. Drink. It's a dog of a night and tomorrow's going to be a dog of a day.

Professor Would you like some water?

Senator No sir.

*The **Professor** goes to the bathroom to adulterate his drink.*

Senator Did you know that according to the law of probability you drink a glass of water and you drink a piece of Napoleon's crap? Perhaps even Mussolini's but more likely Napoleon's on account of he's been dead longer. Attila the Hun's a dead cert he's been gone so long. It's pure probability you take a glass of water you just drink a piece of Attila the Hun's arsehole. I don't drink water. I don't intend to be any part of the Earth's alimentary fucking canal I can tell you that, no sir.

Professor The same probability must surely exist for all liquids.

Senator Whisky's a cleanser. You ever drop a worm in whisky? It'll go stiffer'n a nail in two minutes. If I'm drinking pieces of Mussolini I know they're dead pieces of Mussolini and aren't still swimming around with minds of their own. Now I'm not an educated man, Professor, but I'm a jackdaw when it comes to picking up little facts of knowledge. I don't have any pretensions but I like to think I could hold my own, leastways up to the letter S.

Professor S?

Senator I make it a rule to learn one new word a day. I started when I was fourteen and I'm up to midway through the S's. Want to know today's word? Solifluxion. You know what that means?

Professor The movement of soil due to natural causes.

Senator You got to W already, I bet. Yes sir, the movement of soil due to natural causes. I love knowledge. I'd give a great deal to know all you know.

This the stuff you hump about with you all the time?
Must be quite a few years' work right there. To
tomorrow, Professor. Now the first thing you have to
remember is that you ain't on trial. You're not accused
of anything. You're not here to be accused. If you feel
accused that makes me an unhappy man. Are you
feeling accused?

Professor No, I am feeling persecuted.

Senator Are you now?

Professor Or have I ever been?

Senator That's no accusation, that's an inquiry. Now,
entirely off the record, would you like to tell me what
your answer to that question might be? It seems to me
there are only two answers possible. There is yes and
there is no. There are however some citizens who seem
to think that there is a third answer that doesn't require
the use of either of those two words and I'll tell you,
Professor, they have turned these hearings into one
royal pain in the butt. You know the most times one
man has cited the fifth amendment in the committee
room? Seventy-nine times. He got awfully tired. Now
I'm not here to persuade you to one testimony or
another, Professor, all I ask is that you give us a straight
yes or no so's we can all fly home and get a long
weekend. I haven't seen my wife in a month. Last time
I bought a ticket home I had to spend two extra
sessions trying that jumped-up nigger Robeson for
contempt and missed the damn plane. I'm offering you
a quick dismissal in return for a straight answer to a
straight question. Try one of those little words, yes or
no, by way of experiment.

Professor No?

Senator You're not nor have you ever been?

Professor What then?

Senator We'd go for perjury.

Professor   Ahah. I've been named.

Senator   Three times. I came here tonight to make the situation clear. You're not a politician or a military man; you're not used to kicking about in the mud, then coming up smelling of roses. I'd put you in the same category as some of the movie people we've talked to: the type of person to whom mud sticks. There's a little solifluxion going on right now; the dirt's shifting and it's heading your way. Help us and we'll help you come out clean.

Professor   To come out clean I have to answer yes?

Senator   Yes would be just fine by us. Of course you'd need to couple that with a denunciation of any communist ideals you once held. And a formal condemnation of the Soviets' arms initiative wouldn't do you any harm.

Professor   Would that be all?

Senator   You could show good faith and give us a few names.

Professor   Am I talking to an official Representative of the House Committee for Un-American Activities?

Senator   Well, no one ever put a scare into a rabbit by pretending they haven't got a dog. Guess I'm the dog.

Pause.

Professor   What if I answered yes but refused to condemn communism or to name names, what then?

Senator   Shit, that what you're going to do? I'll tell you in confidence I don't think the hearings proper are going to go on for much longer. You could be our last big fish, Professor, and what a fish. You know just about all there is to know about them photons, atomic structure, cosmology and the Jewish problem. They call you daddy of the H bomb and a true child of the universe. It's in your power to just about wrap this

thing up. We need a man who faced with frankfurters
or hotdogs chose hotdogs. Token American if you like.
After all you chose America.

Professor In my lifetime I have been accused by the
Swiss of being a German fascist, by the Germans of
being a Zionist conspirator, and by the Americans of
being a German fascist, a Zionist conspirator and now a
Soviet communist. I have been an Internationalist and a
diehard patriot. By two magazines in one week I was
called a conscientious objector and a warmonger; both
magazines were reviewing a speech I made to the
Beethoven Appreciation Society of New England. Now
I am asked to stand and say yes or no to a question that
belongs in a fourth grade Latin examination paper.
Answer yes or no so that you can decide if I deserve to
be called an American. I tell you, on or off the record, I
don't care. I never chose America, I was avoiding
Dachau.

Senator Strange how you talk to a good Jew
nowadays, that subject always comes up. Dachau! Same
threat to Democracy we're asking you to fight.

Professor World War Two had nothing to do with
communism.

Senator Nothing to do with . . . ? Whole damn thing
was a Soviet plot!

Professor Fifteen million dead Russians, a Soviet
plot?

Senator They're tricky. Ask yourself this, what's left
of Europe that'll ever be a threat to the Soviets? Round
one's theirs. So, what do you say?

Professor I say you ought to see a psychiatrist. Good
night, Senator.

Senator It'd be a mighty shame if all you stood for
was to get muddied up for the sake of haggling over a
constitutional legality. Don't make the mistake of

treating this like a freshman's debate on civil liberties; there are some who've done that and sounded just fine on the day. One guy got applauded by the fucking stenographer, but he ain't earnt jack shit since. Nor has the stenographer. This thing's got the power to change your life so it's never the same again, worse than a swollen prostate. I glanced through your file. So what about a little co-operation here?

Professor I can make it very simple. I will not, ever, testify.

Senator You're subpoenaed for tomorrow.

Professor I am here to speak at the Conference for World Peace. The date of my subpoena coincided quite beautifully but it will not prevent me from attending. Nor if I had arranged to go fishing would it have prevented me from catching fish.

Senator You ignore a House Committee subpoena and that may be all that's left for you to do. Must be near a lifetime's work there. I heard tell you refuse to have copies made of those, why is that? Be a tragedy if they was to go astray. (*The* **Senator** *stands.*) You're called for nine-thirty. I'll be here around eight to pick you up.

Professor Bring a good book.

Senator I have every faith in the testimony you'll give, Professor. Peace Conference can slug it out in your absence. Waste of time anyway, ain't nobody going to press no button; we got too much invested, I mean think of the real estate. (*The* **Senator** *leaves.*)

The **Professor** *has a thought. He avoids the thought by plunging into the calculus.*

There is a knock on the door.

Professor Who is it?

Actress (*offstage*) You wouldn't believe me.

He opens the door cautiously. The **Actress** *is dressed in a stunning white pleated skirt and dark glasses, a well-worn but expensive fur coat.*

Hi.

Professor Hello.

Actress Are you busy? Only I'm being pursued.

Professor In that case you must come in.

Actress Thank you. This is an awful liberty I know, but I'm very honoured to meet you.

Professor Who is pursuing you?

Actress Just about everybody. I thought you'd be asleep. It's three-thirty. (*Pause.*) Would you like me to go?

Professor No, please.

Actress I had to come and see you before you fly home or I fly west and I've hardly had a moment; I've been shooting all week. My movie. (*She removes her glasses.*) You don't recognise me, do you?

Professor Ahhm. No.

Actress That's wonderful. (*Pause.*) Have I interrupted your work?

Professor No, just some calculations.

Actress What are you trying to calculate?

Professor I am trying to unify the field.

Actress Will it take long?

Professor Another four years perhaps.

Actress Gee.

Professor You are an actress?

Actress Mmhmm.

Professor What is your name?

She goes to the window and points out to the flashing neon.

Professor Ahh. I've heard of her. Is she good?

Actress She tries hard.

Professor Why is she here?

Actress A visit.

Professor Why?

Actress You're famous!

Professor So are you.

Actress I know. We have an awful lot in common.

Professor Because of being famous, everywhere I go people fall over themselves to be with me, like a troupe of clowns chasing an old automobile. Because of fame everything I do is likely to develop into a ridiculous comedy.

Actress You're lucky. Everything I do develops into a nightmare. People throw themselves in front of me and I daren't stop.

Professor Who in particular is pursuing you at this time of night?

Actress Oh, a drama coach and an ex-baseball star, the usual kind of person. I think I lost them. Have I disturbed you?

Professor No, no.

Actress Shall I go?

Professor No, no, no. (*Long pause.*) What kind of movie are you . . .

Actress Shooting.

Professor Shooting?

Actress A crummy one.

Professor Who do you er, act?

Actress I play this girl. She's a what, not a who. She has no name; she's just a figment of some guy's imagination. He just imagines having me around the place you know? I spend the entire movie in the tub or the kitchen or having my skirt blown up round my ears. They fixed up a wind machine beneath a grating out on Fifty-Third; I've been out there since before midnight having my skirt blown up round my goddam ears. I know now why umbrellas give up. So it got to three-thirty and there were about a thousand people cheering each time the fan went wham and the police finally made us pack up so's the milk trucks could get through. And I knew my last chance to see you before you left New York or I died from intimate exposure would be to wake you up in the middle of the night and I told myself go ahead, because if he doesn't understand how you have to wake people up in the middle of the night sometimes, nobody will. I thought What The Hell. Have you ever noticed how what the hell is always the right decision? What did you do tonight?

Professor I er, arrived and then washed and then attempted to derive the tangential vector quantities for αc^2 when the value for t is infinity.

Actress You had a bad night too, huh?

Professor Certainly. I could have been beneath the stars watching a pretty girl have her skirt blown up around her ears.

Actress Would you have watched?

Professor Would you have liked me to?

Actress Yes. It would have embarrassed me. I was upset by the others but they didn't embarrass me. I don't think a girl should go through a thing like that without feeling embarrassed, it doesn't seem natural somehow.

Professor How would I have embarrassed you when they couldn't?

Actress They saw a star doing glamorous things right there on the block, you'd have seen a girl flashing her legs for a bunch of jerks. (*Pause.*) Could I explain something to you?

Professor Certainly, what?

Actress The Theory of Relativity.

Professor All of it?

Actress Just the Specific Theory. The General Theory's a little too complex to go into here don't you think?

Professor Just the Specific?

Actress Mmhmm.

Professor Because it's there?

Actress Because I'm here. Would it really bore you? I'll never have another chance to prove it.

Professor Why do you have to prove it? You know what you know.

Actress But you don't believe me.

Professor If you say you understand Relativity then I believe you.

Actress You're just saying that to avoid seeing me embarrass myself.

Professor Of course not.

Actress You honestly believe I understand Relativity.

Professor Yes.

Actress Swear to God?

Professor Whose God?

Actress Yours.

Professor Prove it. With my God you take no chances. (*He offers her the pad.*)

Actress I'm not theoretical, I demonstrate. I brought a few things. (*She produces an array of objects from her coat pockets, things gathered for the purpose, and demonstrates the following as extravagantly as possible.*) If I make a little mistake I want you to stop me. If I go completely off the rails I think you'd better let me finish. I don't always think along exactly your lines, I mean who does, but I can get the same results. Eventually. That's valid isn't it? Ready?

Professor Go.

Actress Well, first of all you have to know two things. The first thing is that if you drop a copy of *The Brothers Karamazov* in a moving train it doesn't fly backwards and flatten the conductor. It drops relative to the train. That's a very important word, please put it in your vocabulary book. The second thing you have to know is that light absolutely always, whatever speed the flashlight it came from might be travelling, the light absolutely always travels at the same speed in all directions. 186,282 miles per second?

Professor Point 397.

Actress It got faster?

Professor We got more accurate.

Actress Then don't confuse me. Now we have to imagine a man in a car travelling at thirty miles an hour, and a hitchhiker standing by the road waiting for a lift. The driver, as he drives up at thirty miles an hour, throws a stone at the hitchhiker ahead of him at another thirty miles an hour. He's a major league pitcher. So the question is if the car is travelling at thirty miles an hour and a stone is thrown in front of it at thirty miles an hour, what is the speed of the stone when it hits the hitchhiker? Answer, sixty miles an hour. Pretty straightforward. But let's forget the stone and instead imagine the man in the car flashing his headlights to tell the hitchhiker to get the hell out of the way. Does the light from the headlamps travel towards the hitchhiker at 186,282 point . . . ?

Professor 397 . . .

Actress Miles per second plus thirty miles per hour? Answer, no! Because the speed of light is always the same. Did you ever prove that hypothesis?

Professor It was never disproved.

Actress Let's hope it never is.

Professor Amen.

She has by this time dropped, thrown or manœuvred a book, a small flashlight, a magazine with an automobile on the front and a little toy model of Charlie Chaplin. Now she reveals her pièce de résistance, *two little trains, with track.*

Actress Now. Here we go. We have to imagine two locomotives speeding past each other at a hell of a speed. A red one and a green one. The driver of each locomotive has a flashlight which he turns on at the precise moment they pass each other. Now the light from each flashlight travels at the same speed regardless of the speeds of the flashlights themselves, so both flashes expand in all directions just like a single sphere of light. Now the driver of the red locomotive watches the light spread out at the same speed in all directions at once and regardless of the fact he's moving very fast thataway (*She points left.*) . . . he stays with the centre of the sphere of light that came from his flashlight, both flashlights. And if he looks over at the green locomotive he'll see that the driver of the green train has moved thataway (*She points right.*) . . . and is therefore not at the centre of the light any more. I

know you're way ahead of me. Everything's just fine
until you look at it from the point of view of the driver
of the green train. He too, remember, flashed his light
and he too watches it spread out at the same speed in
all directions at once regardless, and so he too stays
with the centre of the sphere of light and looks over to
see the red locomotive has moved like crazy thataway
(*She points left.*) . . . and isn't in the centre of the light
any more. So both drivers think they're the ones in the
centre of the light while the other driver has moved on
past. Question, which one is right? Answer, both of
them. Not only that. I figured out what would happen
if you just stood on the tracks and watched. The light
would stay with you and the trains would both vamoose
and you'd be right too!

Professor That's remarkably. . .

Actress That's not all. If we stand on the tracks a
little longer you know what happens?

Professor We get run over? (*Pause.*) I stay behind
afterwards and clean the blackboard.

Actress I don't like to be patronised.

Professor I'm sorry.

Actress Your apology's accepted. Anyway, if we watch
from the tracks a little longer we see that the distance
between the light and the green train after a few
seconds is the same as the distance between the light
and the red train, but the driver of the green train
thinks his distance from it is much less than the red
train's distance, I mean no distance at all, and vice
versa, the driver of the red train thinks his distance
from the light is less. You know what that means?

Professor Yes.

Actress No you don't. It means that distances
measured are always shorter if you measure them
yourself rather than get someone else to do it. And it's

not just distances, it's time as well. Have you got a watch, can we use it? We have to imagine this room is the universe. (*Turns lights off.*) We begin together somewhere in Space-Time at exactly five o'clock and we synchronise.

Professor   Five o'clock.

Actress   Five o'clock. Now I travel away from you at a heck of a speed, let's say one fifth of the speed of light, and I travel for five minutes and it gets me here. Now my watch says five past five but it isn't very reliable so I look across to check what your watch says and what does it say?

Professor   Five past five.

Actress   Not to me it don't. It says four minutes past five because five minutes past five hasn't reached me yet. I don't see a minute ticked off on your watch until a minute later than you because it takes a minute for me to see your watch because light is taking a minute to get here, see? So now I travel away for another five minutes, put your watch on five more minutes . . . until my watch says ten past five and I look across and your watch says, wait for it, eight minutes past five which means that your watch is getting slower and slower!! Now here comes the really exciting part. I say your watch says eight minutes past five, what do you say your watch says?

Professor   Ten minutes past five.

Actress   But that's what I say mine says. Now here's the thousand dollar question. Remember that if you look at my watch it's going to take the light two minutes to reach you. What do you say my watch says?

Professor   Eight minutes past five? (*Pause.*)

Actress   Which means that I say you're going more slowly than me while you say I'm going more slowly than you.

Professor Beautiful.

Actress Isn't it. So . . . ! (*She turns on the lights.*)
Given a constant frame of reference within which to
experiment according to Galileo's original Principles
and accepting the hypothesis that light always travels at
186,282 point 397 miles per second in all directions at
once . . . the main point I have demonstrated is that all
measurements of Time and Space are necessarily made
relative to the observer, and are not necessarily the same
for two independent observers. That is the Specific
Theory of Relativity. Isn't it?

Professor Yes it is.

She sighs a huge sigh of relief and falls back on the bed.

Actress Now you have to show me your legs.

The **Professor** *rolls his trousers up around his knees.*

Professor I promise never to display these in public if
you promise never to lecture in nuclear physics.

Actress Done.

Professor How far did you get with the General
Theory?

Actress Oh, I know that too, all the way through.
Only I didn't understand a word of it.

Professor You learned it without understanding it?

Actress Mmhmm. It's like riding the subway. I know
where to get on and where to get off but while I'm
travelling I don't know where the hell I am. I suppose
you must, but then you dug all the tunnels. In any case,
I know the premise and the results, that's the main
thing.

Professor That's nothing. Knowledge is nothing
without understanding. Let me tell you this. This watch
we used. My father gave it to me when I was five years
old, anything precious he used to give away. It regulated

the world around me and helped me understand, one
day at a time. Sunrise at five, sunset at nine, dinner at
twelve and father home at seven. Then one week I was
ill in bed, my watch by my side, observing the world
through the little window, and my father brought me
another small gift. It was a little stump of metal about
so long. I asked what it was, was it precious, what
should I do with it, what did it do? My father told me
to find out. Three days I didn't learn what it was; the
world stayed the same, a known quantity, but then on
the third day I reached for my watch from the bedside
table and it jumps. It catches the little piece of metal
and it carries it up. It is a little magnet and it pulled my
world apart. I no longer understood! So I studied, and
now I understand magnetism. I know the truth of
magnetism. This is why you must not pretend to have
grasped the General Theory. You may know a great
deal but without understanding you will never know the
truth.

Actress You mean it's no use knowing how many
beans make ten if you haven't learned to count to five?

Professor Probably, yes.

Actress Well, I don't know if that's what you mean,
but that's how I understand it.

Professor You're too bright for your own good. You
know too much and understand too little.

Actress I understand I was born and that I'm still
living.

Professor So?

Actress So don't talk to me as if I were a child.

Professor Liebchen. . .

Actress Don't patronise me! There was a woman
reporter once who asked me in the middle of an
interview for *Harpers* how long a whale could stay

underwater before it drowned. (*Pause.*) She said it was a kind of intelligence test.

Professor   Whose intelligence was at stake?

Actress   It doesn't matter. What matters is I didn't know and I thought it mattered. So I try to know things, is that so wrong?

Professor   If I told you the moon is made of cheese, would you believe me?

Actress   No.

Professor   If I told you it was made of granite?

Actress   Maybe.

Professor   If I told you I knew for certain?

Actress   I'd believe you.

Professor   So now you know the moon is made of granite?

Actress   Yes.

Professor   But it isn't.

Actress   I only said I knew because you said you knew.

Professor   Precisely, but I was wrong. Knowledge is not truth, it is merely agreement. You agree with me, we agree with someone else, we all have knowledge but get no closer to the truth of the moon. You cannot understand by making definitions, only by turning over the possibilities. It's called thinking. If I say I know, I stop thinking, but so long as I think, I come to understand, I might approach some truth. (*Pause.*) However, something I know, is that there are men, there are such men; I know of greed, I know of hate, I know of evil, but I cannot, I will not, understand these things.

Actress   This is the best conversation I ever had.

He is tired.

Actress Is it over?

Professor I think it had better be.

She rises. He hands her her coat. She doesn't put it on.

Actress A girlfriend and I played a game a few years back. We each made a list of the men it would be nicest to sleep with. You came third on mine.

Professor Third.

Actress Then we worked out how old you are.

Professor And you struck me off.

Actress No, I moved you to the top.

Pause.

Professor No. Thank you for considering me.

Actress You can't just throw me on the streets at this hour.

Professor You are absolutely right. You are welcome to stay. I shall sleep in the bathtub.

Actress That would be absurdly uncomfortable.

Professor A fine American tradition. (*He takes some bedding from the bed.*)

Actress You can't sleep in the bath.

Professor What's good enough for Cary Grant is good enough for me.

Actress Wouldn't it be nice just to share the bed? We don't have to make love. Personally I think you'd be a damn fool not to.

Pause.

Professor I think I have to be a damn fool.

She puts on her coat.

Perhaps I could give you my telephone number. You'd be very welcome to visit me at my home.

Actress Nonsense. I might end up on first name terms with your telephone service but you'd never find time for me.

Professor I have no service. I have a secretary whose first name is still a mystery to me after four years. I have a small house on a large river full of fish which I can't catch and I have a great deal of time to offer.

Actress I'm sorry. I have none to give you beyond now. The little time my work leaves me my husband demands, what he leaves I need for myself, and Dostoievsky steals most of that. I hoped we could just . . . come together, you know, in the middle of all this, for an hour or so.

Professor Then don't go.

She smiles.

But I sleep in the bathtub! If two people do not give each other time, they give each other nothing.

Actress Time is relative too, remember. If we were twins, born at exactly the same time, were exactly the same age, and yet I was to travel away from you and back at some fantastic speed, when I got back I'd be younger than you wouldn't I?

Professor Yes you would.

Actress You proved that. I would be younger, which means the less you move the faster you grow old. It means you've got to keep moving.

Professor I suppose it does.

Actress So then why won't you sleep with me?

Professor Because I could never end up younger.

She moves to the pile of calculus, kneels beside it and embraces it.

Actress You're calculating the shape of space, right?

Professor Absolutely.

Actress When you've finished this you will have expressed the precise nature of the physical universe, right?

Professor So?

She leaves the calculus and touches his leg.

Actress So do it tomorrow. It'll be here. I won't.

Professor No.

He takes his bedding to bathroom. She goes to window.

Actress I wish they'd switch me off.

Professor I prefer to look up.

Actress Stars are too far away. They make me feel small and lonely. Sad.

Professor Me too, small and lonely, but not sad. All who look feel as small and lonely as the rest. Doesn't that make you feel happier?

Actress A little.

Professor Smallness happens and aloneness happens but the miracle is that insignificance doesn't happen. The stars tell us we can walk on the grass, talk to anyone we meet, touch those people, ask anything of them; the stars won't think the worse of us. The stars won't even notice. (*Pause. He fetches the bedding back from the bathroom.*) So, what the hell. (*He sits on the bed, clutching his pillow.*)

She starts to undress. He winds his alarm clock.

Is it late or early?

Actress It's relative. Your watch is just there.

Professor It hasn't told me the time since I was seven years old.

Actress Did you drop it?

Professor No, I picked it up, with a large electromagnet.

She shows him her watch.

They continue undressing.

There is a loud knocking on the door.

Ballplayer Open the door you dumb broad, I know you're in there! (*Pause.*) You in there? (*Three thumps.*)

Actress You are, I'm not.

Professor Who is it?

Actress Just a fan.

Professor Do all your fans follow you so persistently?

Actress Only those I marry.

Ballplayer (*offstage*) You want me to go get a pass key? I only have to sign my name and the nightman'd open this door damn fast, you know that.

Professor He is famous?

Actress He hit safely in fifty-six consecutive games with an average of four hundred and thirty-five. He's God. He can open most doors . . .

Heavy thump.

One way or the other.

Professor Should I let him in?

Actress No, he's angry.

Professor You think if we keep the door closed he'll get happy?

Ballplayer (*offstage*) You hiding yourself in the john? I'm going to look in the john. There's no place to hide. I'm going to kill you.

Professor Would he harm you with me here?

Actress (*with a glance at the window*) No, he'd harm me with you on the sidewalk.

Three thumps on the door.

I think he's just angry, not livid, the way he's banging.

Professor How can you tell?

Thump.

Actress He's not using his head.

Professor I'll go and talk to him.

Actress Wait until I've figured what mood he's in . . .

Another thump dissuades him from opening the door.

Professor *Ja, was ist das denn, was kann ich für ihn tun?*

Pause.

Ballplayer (*offstage*) So you finally slept with the delicatessen. You speak English?

Professor *Ich kann nicht lügen.* Yes, I do.

Ballplayer So is my wife in there with you?

Professor It's five o'clock in the morning.

Ballplayer You a man of honour?

Professor I hope so.

Ballplayer You'd tell me straight if she was there?

Professor If you ask me straight, I will tell you, yes.

Pause.

Ballplayer I'll tell you what I'm going to do. I'm going to count to ten. If she's in there then you open the door and let me get at her, OK? If she's not there you tell me so and as a man of honour I'll believe you and leave you to sleep. OK. I'm going to count to ten.

Pause. The **Professor** *breathes deeply.*

Actress You never counted past three in your life, you dumb ox!

Ballplayer (*offstage*) Shit.

Actress One, two, three, home; that's as far as you ever bothered to go.

Silence.

Professor You think he's gone?

Biggest thump yet as he throws himself at the door.

Actress Uh uh. But he's in quite good control; you almost had a conversation. I'm going to let him in. Lock yourself in the bathroom.

Professor Certainly not.

Actress OK. If he goes like that (*She hits her head with her fist.*) . . . then make straight for the elevator. I'll be way in front of you. If he cracks his knuckles let him speak.

He is throwing himself at the door regularly. The **Actress** *carefully sets herself up to open it for him to fly into the room.*

She opens it wide. He is nowhere to be seen.

He then steps casually into the doorway.

Ballplayer You think I'm dumb or some. . .

She throws the door in his face.

Actress Yes, I think you're dumb.

Ballplayer You crazy? You made my nose bleed.

Professor I'll get a damp cloth.

He exits into the bathroom. The **Actress** *sits down.*

Ballplayer Why'd you pull a stunt like that?

Actress What happens when you're angry?

Ballplayer I hit out.

Actress And what happens when you see blood?

Ballplayer You know I go limp, I can't help it.

Actress That's all right, honey, I prefer you this way.

Ballplayer I'm still angry.

Actress I know, but listen to this. If you so much as make a move towards that old man then be warned, I'll take off through the door and that's the last you'll see of me for a long time.

Ballplayer That's a very big joke. I want to see my wife I just go to the movies. I want to see my wife's underwear I just walk down to the corner like all the other guys.

*The **Professor** returns with a face cloth.*

Professor Would you like this where. . .?

*The **Ballplayer** snatches it.*

Ballplayer My nose never bled before. I got cracked on the nose once by a high inside fastball and the pitcher's nose bled.

Professor Down your back I think it's meant to go.

Ballplayer So you got screwed by another shrink?

Actress He's not a shrink, he's a friend, and we were talking.

Ballplayer Talking at five in the morning?

Professor It's hard to believe perhaps. . .

Ballplayer No, it's not hard to believe. If she can talk through the entire World Series she can talk until five any morning. Why you got no clothes on?

The **Professor** *has no shoes or shirt.*

Professor It's a dog of a night.

Ballplayer Ain't it? What sort of therapy do you do?

Professor I'm a physicist.

Ballplayer He mean massage?

Actress OK, you were right the first time. He's a shrink.

Ballplayer Pity, I think I bust my shoulder. OK, get your coat.

Actress I'll follow you when I've finished talking.

Ballplayer I said get your coat! (*Pause.*) OK, finish. Tell her what Floyd would have said.

Professor Floyd?

Actress Freud.

Ballplayer She's been to a dozen shrinks. She tells you how she hated her mother and so can't have stable relationships, then you tell her the reason she can't have stable relationships is because she hated her mother, and she pays you fifty dollars and she comes back next week until you make a pass and she goes and finds another shrink. I seen it all before, me and Floyd we're old buddies.

Actress Fer-oid.

Ballplayer One shrink told her she'd got a father fixation for this man Floyd. You guys are driving her nuts.

Professor I'm not a therapist.

Ballplayer I've met her mother and let me tell you, she's easy to hate. Anyone who hates her mother, there's nothing wrong with them.

Actress Stepmother.

Ballplayer I hate you guys, bunch of. . .

Actress Sit down and shut up!

He shuts up, but will not sit.

The Professor is not a psychiatrist, he's an old friend of mine.

Ballplayer Intellectual?

Actress We have never even touched.

Ballplayer She has two types of friend.

Actress The type he doesn't understand and the type he assaults.

Ballplayer I think you're a man of honour; I've got a nose for that sort of thing. Go ahead, talk smart. (*He sits and opens a pack of gum. Looks at card, discards it.*)

Actress Where were we?

Professor Mmm?

Ballplayer You were discussing her head.

Actress As it happens we were discussing the shape of the physical universe.

Ballplayer Easy ones first, huh?

Actress If you'd like to contribute I suppose we could discuss something you know about but that would limit us to the last nine World Series and the names of the Seven Dwarves.

Ballplayer Shift!

Actress Go screw.

Ballplayer One . . .

Actress The shape of the universe.

Ballplayer . . . two . . .

Professor I think this is not the best time.

Ballplayer . . . three . . .

Actress Please. He's still angry. Try four.

Ballplayer Home! The man don't want to talk. He don't have nothing to say, so get off your butt and come home.

Actress Truman or Eisenhower?

Pause. The **Ballplayer** *sits.*

Please, the shape of the universe or something.

Professor It's not important; you have things to discuss.

Actress We had a discussion last month, about the presidential candidates and their policies. To underline his points about *détente*, he broke my Russian doll with a baseball bat.

Ballplayer You embarrassed the man now. She's right, I hit out. We discussed it though; it ain't purposeful. (*He moves away.*) Go ahead, talk smart.

Actress Please.

Professor Well . . . The shape of the universe has to be considered in four-dimensional terms with Time as the fourth dimension. (*He is distracted by the* **Ballplayer** *swinging an imaginary baseball bat.*) . . . Therefore the shape of the universe is impossible to visualise; it can only be imagined.

Actress We have to use our imaginations, can you imagine that?

Professor Er, the universe has no boundaries . . .

Actress It's infinite!

Professor No. Space has no boundaries but neither is it infinite. That is our starting point.

The **Ballplayer** *opens another pack of gum, looks at card* *and discards it. He sticks his chewed gum somewhere unobtrusive.*

Consider one dimension first. Consider length without breadth or width. As a model, a very thin length of rope.

Actress Or a shoelace?

Professor A shoelace if you like.

She unties one of the **Ballplayer's** *shoes.*

Ballplayer Hey, that's a Piper's Brogue shoelace, you can only get those with the shoes.

Actress Don't be a baby, this is science.

Ballplayer She thinks I'm stupid but it's just I watch TV a lot, you know?

Actress Length. No breadth or width, hardly.

Professor Thank you. Now considered in one-dimensional terms this shoelace is obviously not infinite in length, but it does have boundaries; it has two ends. To make it resemble Space it must have no boundary so what must we do with the shoelace?

The **Ballplayer** *snatches the lace.*

Ballplayer How about using it to tie up your shoe?

Professor Very close. You must tie a knot, get rid of the ends.

The **Actress** *snatches it back and ties a knot, tugging it tight.*

Actress A shoelace without infinite length, or boundaries. A circle!

Professor Bravo. But remember, a one-dimensional circle. It is really a rather unusual straight line.

Ballplayer It's a useless fucking shoelace, I know that.

Professor   Now let us think one step further, in two dimensions. Let us think of something that has length and breadth but no width. What would be a suitable model?

Actress   A sheet of paper.

The **Ballplayer** *pops gum. She glares at him.*

Ballplayer   Sorry. She hates that sound.

Actress   We made a pact.

Ballplayer   I don't pop gum, she don't pop nembutal.

The **Actress** *takes a page of her shooting script and tears it out.*

Actress   Length and breadth, no width.

Professor   Now, is it infinite?

Actress   No. But it has boundaries all round the edge.

Professor   So how do we make it without boundaries?

Actress   Stretch it out? Keep stretching?

Professor   No, that would make it infinite.

The **Ballplayer** *pops gum.*

Ballplayer   I did it without thinking.

Actress   Is there anything you do any other way?

Ballplayer   Pardon me for breathing.

Actress   That's the only thing. Your entire life is a reflex action.

Professor   The question is how can an object existing on two planes be finite but have no boundaries?

Actress   I give up.

Professor   You work it out, then we go on.

She thinks. The **Ballplayer** *blows a bubble.*

Actress Don't you dare. (*She holds out her hand, he gives her the gum, with bubble.*) A bubble, curl it up and make it into a bubble, a ball, a sphere.

Professor Yes. But a sphere in two dimensions, not three.

Actress How can balls come in two dimensions?

Ballplayer Balls come in lots of dimensions. There's beach balls, basketballs, baseballs, right?

Actress You dumb ox.

Ballplayer 'Don't you call me no ox.' That's a joke. Doberman says that. You watch Bilko?

Actress The universe is like a baseball!

Professor Like the surface of a baseball, as if it had no centre, only the leather surround.

Ballplayer A hollow baseball.

Professor Exactly.

Ballplayer See, the shape of the universe is like a baseball, only bigger, natch. Like we're in a baseball.

Professor Not exactly in, no. On.

Ballplayer Oh, right. Gravitational pull.

Actress I got it. Like we can think of this planet in two dimensions: North–South and East–West, then its surface has no boundaries but it isn't infinite.

Professor Right. Now the next step is impossible to visualise. We are in three dimensions and we have to start with a real sphere, with length, breadth, and width. A solid baseball. It is finite of course, but it does have boundaries. Imagine a baseball without boundaries and you are in the fourth dimension.

Ballplayer You got a baseball without boundaries and you got no chance of a home run, I know that.

Professor From a line to a circle, from a circle to a sphere, from a sphere to . . . the shape of the universe.

Actress Wow. What? Say it again, say it again.

Professor The universe is in constant motion through Time. You can come closest if you try to imagine turning something absolutely solid inside out, and keep turning it inside out for ever.

Actress Wow.

Ballplayer Bullshit. I've told you what I think. I think it's round, like everything else in nature, the sun, moon, flowers, are all based on a circle, you know that? Like the world. I don't know what shape you two geniuses think the old world is but me and Columbus think it's the same shape as a baseball which is a damn lucky thing for the States because if it wasn't for Columbus we'd all be Indians, you ever think of that? (*Pause.*) Get your coat.

Actress I'm not coming.

Ballplayer Why not?

Actress Because you're an idiot. Answer me one question. How long can a whale stay underwater before it drowns?

Ballplayer You expect me to say for ever but I ain't that stupid, a whale ain't no fish. It breathes like you talk, out the top of its head. Two, three minutes, right?

Actress See, he bothered to answer. At least I didn't bother to answer.

Professor Is he right?

Actress No. A whale can stay under for forty-five minutes if it wants to. I looked it up.

Professor You bothered to look it up?

Ballplayer Here! (*He throws her her coat.*)

Actress I'm not coming.

Ballplayer I ain't angry.

Actress I'm tired.

Ballplayer I have to talk to you.

Actress There's nothing to talk about.

Ballplayer You spend all night whoring around in front of a coupla hundred bozos and that's nothing to talk about?

Actress You see this, it's a smile. It doesn't mean I'm happy, it means I'm smiling. That's what actresses do and that's what I am.

Ballplayer You enjoy men looking up your legs for three hours?

Actress I hate it.

Ballplayer Then quit.

Actress The only thing I hate more than a man looking at my legs is a man expecting me to wear them out cooking him TV dinners.

The **Professor** *goes into the bathroom. The* **Ballplayer** *pops gum.*

You remember my first orgasm?

Ballplayer Yep.

Actress Afterwards I lay in the dark, utterly exhausted, hoping you might light me a cigarette and what did I hear? Pop. That's all I hear now, pathetic little explosions, that's all you give me.

Ballplayer You want a divorce?

The **Professor** *returns for his pad and goes back to the bathroom.* You want to finish it?

Pause.

Actress No.

Ballplayer Then come home. You come home, honey, or I swear I'll go get me a lawyer and I'll disappear so's you can't find me for a change. Bob Dalrymple, he gave me the name of a good man. Look, I wrote it down. I phoned this man. He said with the reputation you got I'd have no trouble at all. He said it'd be a pleasure.

Actress You phoned a lawyer?

Ballplayer You ain't been home for two weeks.

Actress OK.

Ballplayer You coming home?

Actress Mmhmm.

Ballplayer OK.

The **Professor** *enters again.*

Professor Excuse me, I have to get this. . .

Ballplayer It's OK, we're leaving.

Actress I have to use the bathroom first.

Ballplayer OK.

She goes into bathroom.

Ballplayer Baby, leave the door.

She leaves the door ajar. The men sit on the bed, side by side.

Ballplayer You chew gum?

Professor No. (*He takes a piece.*) Thank you.

The **Ballplayer** *takes out the card.*

Ballplayer Huh. Who the hell's Willy McCormack? You ever heard of Willy McCormack?

Professor No.

Ballplayer You see, some punk kid thinks he's a bigshot, they put him on a bubblegum card. (*He discards it.*) You know how many bubblegum series I been in? Thirteen. Thirteen series. I been in Chigley's Sporting Greats, I been in Pinky's World Series Stars 1936, 1937, 1939, 1942, 1944, 1945, 1949, and 1951. I been in Tip-Top Boy's Best Baseball Tips showing how best to pitch, swing, deadstop and slide, and I been Hubbly Bubbly's Baseball Bites best all-rounder nine years running. So no, hey! Hold on. That's thirteen series but . . . twenty-one separate editions all told. And how many kids you know collect? Card for card it must run into millions. I must be stuck in albums from here to the Pacific. World wide. They give gum to little chink kids, don't they? You liberate them one day, they're making swaps next day. I saw on TV they don't take beads and junk up the Amazon no more, they take instant coffee and bubblegum. I could go into a little village in Africa that's hardly seen a white man and they'd say 'Hey, big hitter sit down and have some coffee.' This fame thing's enough to give you the heebies, I can tell you. Thirteen series. Chigley's, Pinky's, Hubbly's and Tip-Top. That's some bubblegum.

Professor I was on Lucky Strike Great Scientific Achievements. (*Pause.*) It's not much though, compared to . . .

Ballplayer Thirteen series.

Professor Thirteen series.

Ballplayer Twenty-one separate cards. You got a claim though, somebody must have heard of you. You just hope they never start recognising you on the streets, that's hell, I tell you. But I ain't complaining. I ain't bought a drink since 1943, no sir. You OK, honey?

Actress (*offstage*) I'm OK.

Ballplayer You like my wife?

Professor She's very intelligent.

Ballplayer You don't think she's beautiful?

Professor Also.

Ballplayer You ask her here?

Professor I think she was feeling lonely with all those people.

Ballplayer Then she should have come home. I like you, I don't believe there could have been any funny business, but let me tell you: both of you, you're smart enough with all that science talk but it don't mean nothing compared to feelings, you know that? I could kill a man, you know? If she ever got it down to one. You know, I get so tightened up, like just before a game, whenever I'm not alone with her. I get so mad because even the team, my old team, they'd rather stare at her than gab about old times. They treat her like a star or something. I'll tell you, never put a woman up on a pedestal, it's too easy for her to kick your teeth down your throat. You know what she needs. She needs a thousand people touching her all of the time, she needs to be alone all of the time also. She's crazy, except when she's with me, then she's whole, you know, peaceful. Except she don't see it. I get so tightened up, like I used to waiting to run into the stadium except now it's all tunnel, there's no . . . (*He tries to indicate the stadium, the sun, the crowds. He takes up his imaginary bat. He takes a swing.*) Nyah!

Actress Honey, steady.

Ballplayer Baby?

Actress I'm OK.

Ballplayer You bleeding again?

Actress Will you please leave me alone so I can pull myself together.

Ballplayer If I did you think she could?

There is a clink of glass on enamel from the bathroom, then a loud crash.

The men leap up.

Baby!

She enters.

Actress OK. I'm OK. (*She passes out.*)

*The **Ballplayer** picks her up.*

Professor Put her to bed. I shall get a doctor.

Ballplayer No, she does this all the time. You fetch a doctor and she'll give you hell.

Professor But she might be ill.

Ballplayer Yeh, she's ill, but she's OK. She always faints in strange bathrooms; she's anaemic. She bleeds, you know? She's loose inside. She can't keep a baby in after it gets so big. They keep trying to tighten her up, she keeps getting loose again. A baby could kill her 'cos to keep it they'd have her made so tight it couldn't come out natural, you know? Something like that. So she feels really bad most of the time.

Professor I think we ought to get a doctor.

Ballplayer She always has one she trusts, until he fucks her over and she has to find another. (*He finds a card in her coat.*) Call him direct, from the lobby.

Professor Keep her warm, or whatever you do. (*The **Professor** leaves.*)

Ballplayer Let me tell you, you, you may be all bright lights on the outside but on the inside you fell down from up there and hit the street. Inside you're damaged, you're broken and bruised, until I don't want to love you any more. How can I make love to a wound? Nothing heals if you fuck around. If there's something wrong with you it's no good peck, peck, pecking at it; you'll just end up all feather and bone. (*He looks over at the neon.*) You think that's you, you fucking mess, you think that's you? (*He swings an imaginary bat, tosses an imaginary ball in the air and smashes it as hard and far as he can.*)

She comes to.

Actress Honey?

Ballplayer (*gently*) You did it again.

Actress I'm OK.

Ballplayer You're a mess.

Actress Thanks.

Ballplayer Sorry. I really piss you off, don't I?

Actress You're my mirror. I see all the little things you do as in a mirror.

Ballplayer You see you in me?

Actress No, I see you.

Ballplayer Not a hell of a lot you don't. You mean you and me are a lot alike? (*He finds tablets in her coat and gives her two.*)

Actress We're not at all alike. It's just that things you do strike chords in me that resonate so deeply I don't want to lose you. I'm afraid of never hearing them again.

Ballplayer We sound the same?

Actress I only wish you weren't so stupid.

Ballplayer You think I'm a mirror, you sound like I sound like, we're the same, we're different. You spend your whole life talking bull and I'm stupid!

Actress I'm trying to communicate with you without resorting to batting averages. I'm trying to tell you how I love you.

Ballplayer Not a hell of a lot.

Actress Not how much or how little, how.

Ballplayer How?

Actress In my way.

Ballplayer What about my way?

Actress What's that?

Ballplayer My way. My way. What I want. (*He breaks off for gum.*)

Enter the **Professor.**

Professor Doctor Steinberg is fishing in New Jersey.

Actress I'm fine. Really.

The **Professor** *gathers some of his things.*

Professor I had a small word with the night porter, he's going to find me a room on another floor. No, stay, please. You sleep, get well. Be my guest.

Ballplayer Hey. See what I mean. Every five or six packs. Here.

The **Professor** *takes the card.*

Professor Thank you. Toothbrush. (*He goes into the bathroom.*)

Actress Do you still want a child?

The **Ballplayer** *shakes his head. Blows gum, stops himself, sucks it back in.*

Ballplayer I want the one we already had.

Actress I was under contract. What if I was careful?

Ballplayer I don't care no more. (*He clambers onto the bed and eventually curls up, his head in her lap, having stuck his gum behind his ear.*)

Actress It might be a son.

Ballplayer And it might be a fucking mess.

Actress I'm highly strung, not a hereditary disease. I want to be pregnant.

Ballplayer It'd never get born.

Actress This one will.

Ballplayer It'd tear you up. What they don't tear up, you tear up yourself.

Actress Not all my life. Something's going to give. I want . . . if it happens . . . a daughter. A son?

He is asleep.

Honey, I think I am. Honey?

*The **Professor** crosses with his sponge bag.*

They look at each other.

She gestures, clutching faintly for something she doubts she'll ever attain. Her hand goes to her face and she begins to weep.

*The **Professor** picks up his calculus, clutches it to him, and leaves.*

Act Two

Morning. The **Actress** *is alone, asleep.*

There is a quiet knock on the door.

Senator (*offstage*) Professor? (*The* **Senator** *enters with a small breakfast tray.*) I brought you a little breakfast Professor. It's eight o'clock.

The **Actress** *wakes up and focuses on the* **Senator**. *He gapes.*

I do apologise, I must have gotten out at the wrong floor. All these rooms do look the same. (*He notices some of the* **Professor**'s *things. He checks the door number.*) This is room six-fourteen? Professor's room?

Actress He moved. I don't know where.

Senator Has anyone ever told you, you could be the splitting image . . .

Actress I know, if I was six years younger and took more care.

Senator Right.

She takes pills.

Will he be coming back? Only I had arranged to meet him.

Actress You'll find him in the lobby.

Senator Would you mind if I used the washroom?

Actress He's not in there. I told you he took another room.

Senator Well I can tell you that wherever he is he's certainly shot up in my estimation. Do you mind if I wait?

Actress Not if you don't mind my throwing up.

Senator You've taken a dislike to me I can tell. It's my fault, I have been insensitive. Please accept this breakfast as a little solatium from me to you. A solatium is a small gift in recompense for inconvenience or wounded feelings. (*The* **Senator** *puts the tray beside the bed.*) You know, you could be sisters. Must be kind of advantageous for a girl like you.

Actress Are you a colleague of the Professor's?

Senator We're just good friends. You could say that he and I are both seekers after knowledge in our own ways. We pick up little things and turn them over in our minds. Word for today is Solipsism; you want to know what solipsism means?

Actress It's the belief that only you exist, that everything else exists in your imagination.

Senator College girl too huh? Well, notice you said *you* meaning me rather than *me* meaning you. You explained that only *I* exist, not that only *you* exist. That kind of gives the theory weight from my point of view.

Actress Lucky for you I'm not a solipsist.

Senator Why's that?

Actress I can't imagine inventing you.

Senator Would you pass me the toast?

Actress Imagine some.

Senator I did. There it is.

Actress Imagine it closer why don't you?

Senator Because that's why I invented you.

There is a knock on the door.

Actress Come in.

Enter **Professor**.

Senator Good morning, Professor, I brought you up some breakfast. I been having a little chat about solipsism with your college friend here. I'm deeply committed to the concept, I should be after all I invented it.

Professor Have you been disturbed?

Actress Profoundly.

Professor Would you leave now, please.

Senator Can't be done, Professor, we got business first. I was going to remind you of the mud soliflucting in your direction but it seems like you're involved in what could be a major landslide right here. I mean I could have been the bellboy; you'd have had a fleet of photographers hanging on your door right now. Lucky for you I'm a man of the world.

Actress Who is this?

Professor A representative of the people. I am supposed to appear before the Un-American Committee today. He wishes to compose my testimony for me.

Actress Then tell him to go screw.

Professor Go screw.

Actress Goes for me too.

Senator Are you willing to testify?

Professor No.

Senator Then I have to warn you that you may be subject to an investigation into your political activities. I have reason to suspect you of conspiracy to overthrow the US government.

Actress He's got to be kidding.

Senator Sounds good though don't it? That's how it goes in the book. This is all by the book. The book is what they pay me for.

Actress Is he for real?

Senator You think I'm not?

Actress I think you're fat.

Senator You're very charming.

Actress You're very fat.

Senator Would you like me to call the vice squad?

Professor I think we should discuss this in the lobby.

The **Professor** *opens the door. The* **Heavy** *reaches in and closes it.*

Professor Oh wey.

Actress Oh God.

Senator I told you we had business first. I have here a warrant issued by the Department of Defense authorising me to search your room and belongings for any material or artefact that might be deemed harmful to the United States of America. And this here's a warrant to confiscate any such material under the State Protection Act of 1894. (*He begins to search the room.*)

Actress Why don't you stop him?

Professor Please, don't get involved.

Actress I am involved.

Professor You're not!

Actress I demand to know what's going on! Why are you doing this?

Senator Now that is a question the Professor has not thought to ask.

Actress Then ask him! Then I'll ask him! Why?

Senator It's very simple. The Atomic Energy Commission comes under review by Congress next month. Another few bright young senators are going to try to put the lid on the Nevada Tests, in spite of the fact that we have to match the Soviet initiative. The President needs to be backed by top men. You're the Top Man.

Professor There are a dozen others far more advanced than I in that particular field.

Senator Who the hell's heard of them?

Actress I have. Whatsisname, and Oppenheimer!

Senator Oppenheimer's name casts a shadow of doom since Nagasaki, besides why pass the buck when you can throw it to the end of the line? The world chooses its own heroes. There's no shadow on the pristine world of theory, no strains of Armageddon in $E = mc^2$, even if mc^2 does equal one fuck of a big bang. Where is it?

Actress What does he want? What do you want?

Senator Just a bunch of stuff that was lying around here.

Actress He wants your work? But that's not subversive.

Senator Keeps it mighty close though.

Actress Because it's priceless, not secret! This is some sort of plot!

Senator One thing I've learned about communists is they think everything's a plot. You give 'em a parking ticket and they think it's a plot. Best way to catch a communist is to give them three tickets in a row and if they start picking up the phone listening for taps you know you got one.

Actress How do you know if they pick up the phone?

Senator You tap it. They ain't paranoid, they's communist!

Professor Room 209. On the bed.

The **Senator** *makes to go. The* **Actress** *stops him.*

Actress Now hold on. If you take the calculus you'll check it and return it, won't you? It will be returned, won't it?

Senator Well, these things take time.

Actress But there are no copies. It will be safe? I mean you are acting officially aren't you?

Senator Well good grief, if I wasn't there'd be nothing to stop me destroying the stuff altogether.

Actress You don't suspect him of anything at all. This is just blackmail. And you just stand there. Report him!

Senator Who to?

Actress FBI, CIA, I don't care, NBC, what's to stop us?

Senator Common sense I should think. A little adverse publicity might not do a girl like you any harm, but think of the Professor's position.

Professor I'll fetch it.

Actress No! He has no sense of priorities, don't trust him. Do what he wants, but don't risk your work.

Professor My work is nothing.

Actress Your work is priceless!

The **Professor** *leaves. The* **Senator** *nods to the* **Heavy** *to follow.*

Senator Follow him. Meet me in the lobby.

The **Heavy** *leaves.*

Actress Who are you?

Senator I'm a julep-drinking, nigger-whipping, Louisiana boy. This isn't a game. We're talking about the survival of the free world. We do need his support.

Actress And for that you'd steal his soul?

Senator Ain't difficult once you've sold your own. My orders are to find his work, take it and sit on it. Then I get a call and I hand it back or I shred the damn thing.

Actress Do you realise what it is you're talking about? It isn't just the culmination of a man's life work although Lord knows . . . It's a set of calculations that come close to describing the shape of Space/Time. He's almost unified the fields. If you'd just let him finish he'll have calculated how it all fits. How everything is. Doesn't that strike you as important?

Senator You ain't talking to green corn you know. I've given a great deal of thought as to the importance of those documents and I came to the conclusion that the shape of Space/Time is of fuck-all importance to any of us. It's just paper, otherwise why would he throw it all away?

Actress He trusts you.

Senator Nobody's that dumb.

Actress He's weak.

Senator Well, it's a dog-eat-dog world.

Actress Please don't destroy it.

Senator You know it's uncanny. At times you er . . . you've really studied the lady haven't you?

Actress I could let you have money.

Senator You trying to bribe a US senator?

Actress Yes.

Senator Takes a lot of dollars to buy a man. Where'd a girl like you get money like that?

Actress I'm not a girl.

Senator I was being polite. Well, you've tried

appealing to my back pocket and to my intelligence. You got any more little persuasions you want to try?

She laughs.

Pause.

Actress Maybe.

Senator I beg your pardon, what was that?

Pause.

Actress All right.

Senator Do I understand you correctly? In return for my leaving you the calculus you're offering me sexual favours?

Actress A sexual favour. I mean, what the hell? (*Pause. She locks the door.*)

After all it's not me is it? It's her you want. (*She clambers onto the bed and begins to undo his trousers.*)

He hits her. Expertly. One blow to the head, one to the belly. She is thrown back on the bed.

He dresses himself.

Senator I ain't ever paid for it in my life, least of all with my integrity. Did I hurt you? (*He goes to the window for air.*) My son had her picture on his wall! I whupped his ass! They call her a goddam goddess. I mean shit, she's mortal ain't she? I mean she only got where she is same way as you. (*He comes closer to her.*) Listen, girl like you gotta look after her little body. Your little body ain't worth no pile of paper. (*He sits.*) If I hurt you I apologise. Nothing personal.

The door handle moves. Somebody knocks. The **Senator** *opens the door.*

Enter the **Ballplayer.**

Well if it ain't the big hitter himself! What the hell are you doing here?

Ballplayer I don't believe it. Every time I turn my back there's a different man in my wife's room.

Senator Your wife's . . .? Oh shit.

Actress Sweetheart . . .

Ballplayer Who's this?

Senator I guess it was time I was moving along.

Ballplayer Is he OK, honey?

Senator (*backing out*) It's an honour to meet you, sir, I've been a fan for years. Game just hasn't been the same without you.

Actress Don't let him leave.

The **Ballplayer** *runs across and blocks the door.*

Ballplayer Something happen while I was out?

Senator Nothing at all.

Ballplayer Honey?

Actress No.

Ballplayer You sure?

Actress Oh God. (*She curls up and cuts herself off.*)

Ballplayer Baby, what do you want me to do? Baby? (*He crosses, concerned.*)

The **Senator** *moves to the door.*

Hey! Sit down.

Senator Look, I simply came to speak to the Professor, whose room this is, as he'll tell you . . .

Ballplayer Listen, my wife asked me to keep you here. Until I find out why, your choice is to sit down unaided or lie down with assistance.

Senator Are you threatening me?

Ballplayer No, I have never had to hit an intelligent man.

*The **Senator** considers, then sits.*

*Enter the **Professor** with the calculus.*

Who's he? She don't want him to leave.

*The **Professor** ties a cord around the calculus and hands it to the **Senator**. The **Actress** groans and takes a sharp breath.*

Professor Now please, go away.

Senator It'd be a pleasure.

Ballplayer Get your butt back in the chair!

Senator Can you talk some sense into this man?

Professor I'm told it's not possible.

Senator Listen, we're all civilised human beings . . .

Ballplayer Baby, you want me to keep this man here? What he do, honey?

Professor He did nothing, I promise you. His business was with me. Please, let him go.

Ballplayer Honey?

Actress Let him go. All of you go.

Ballplayer You a man of honour?

Senator I'm a solipsist.

Ballplayer OK.

Their shake hands.

What's a solipsist, remind me.

Senator I believe that only I exist. All the rest of you exist only in my imagination.

*The **Ballplayer** laughs.*

Ballplayer That's stupid. I exist.

Senator Sure you do, but only in my head.

Ballplayer OK, if we only exist in your head then how come we were here last night without you?

Senator You weren't.

Ballplayer Bullshit. We were here before you arrived even.

Senator Prove it.

Ballplayer If I don't exist how come I'm arguing?

Senator I like to argue.

The **Ballplayer** *thinks.*

Ballplayer Don't go away! (*The* **Ballplayer** *goes out and closes door behind him.*)

Ballplayer (*offstage*) You there?

Senator Of course.

Ballplayer (*offstage*) Right, let me tell you something. I ain't with you and I still exist!

Senator Prove it.

The door half opens.

Ballplayer Oh no!

Door closes.

Senator You're nothing!

Ballplayer (*offstage*) No I ain't!

Senator Yes you are!

Ballplayer (*offstage*) Then what am I doing now? If I'm in your imagination you should be able to tell me what I'm doing.

Senator Swinging an imaginary baseball bat?

The **Ballplayer** *enters.*

Ballplayer How the fuck did you know that? I do thousands of things when you ain't around. I drink coffee, I screw around, I go to movies . . .

Senator No you don't, I only think you do.

Ballplayer What about everyone else?

Senator All in here.

Ballplayer What about everyone who lived before you, everyone who's dead?

Senator I killed 'em.

Silence. The **Actress,** *the* **Professor** *and the* **Ballplayer** *look at the* **Senator.** *The* **Senator** *heads for the door.*

Now remember, you all be on your best behaviour now. The folk like to think they're in the hands of gods. That's why I dreamed up you special people.

The **Senator** *leaves. Long pause.*

Ballplayer I'm still here! I can hold my own intellectually, I just have to concentrate.

The **Actress** *stirs.*

Baby. Can you talk?

Actress Of course I can talk.

Ballplayer You better, honey? Did you wonder where I was? I went for a long walk and I had a good think. I finally decided what's best for me to do.

Actress You lost your work.

Professor And I have lost my shoes.

Actress You let him walk all over you!

Professor I have no shoes!

Actress 209.

Professor Ah. (*The* **Professor** *exits, barefoot.*)

Ballplayer I got it all figured out. I had a long walk. You want a kid, I want a kid. We get on most of the time but the problem is most of the time you can't stand me, right? And why can't you stand me, because I'm stupid. I admit it. I'm proud of it but it drives you nuts. Well, let me reveal to you a secret, I am not genuinely stupid, I just enjoy being stupid. I have always enjoyed being stupid. From an early age I have revelled in stupidity. Let me tell you another thing, I am also as stubborn as a mule, which explains why when you told me so often to smarten up and left books on the TV accidently I'd never even read the ones that looked kind of interesting. But I took a walk and I had a long think. I've been thinking and what I've decided is that if you still want me to smarten up, well I figure you're worth it. (*Pause.*) So what I figure is while you finish your movies I'll sit right down and read a few good books. You can quiz me. And I'll get rid of the TV so there's no more TV and no more TV dinners. If you like, no more ball games. You come home, I'll smarten up. We'll have a couple of kids. No more gum. (*Pause. He removes gum and sticks it somewhere.*)

Actress Honey, it's over. You'd better call up your lawyer friend.

Ballplayer You think so?

Actress Yeh.

Ballplayer Yes, I think so too. Maybe I'm that smart. (*He puts on his jacket.*) You take some advice? You got to figure out what you want.

Actress I don't want you.

Ballplayer What do you want?

Actress I don't want to want.

Ballplayer Yeh, but what do you want?

She weeps, or comes close to it, but stops him going to her.

Actress I want to go, do you understand? I want to go.

The **Ballplayer** *tries to leave. He retrieves his gum and opens a fresh pack.*

Ballplayer You want some gum?

Actress I don't chew gum.

Ballplayer Oh yeh. (*He leaves.*)

The **Actress** *breathes deeply and braces herself.*

She takes a box of tissues, takes a handful beneath the bedclothes and puts them into herself. She throws back the clothes.

She has been bleeding. Her slip is wet, the bedclothes stained red.

She gets up, covers the stain carefully, picks up her dress and shoes, and walks unsteadily into the bathroom, shoes in her hand.

Enter the **Professor**, *shoes in hand.*

Professor Hello?

A noise from the bathroom.

He sits with his pad but gets nowhere.

I want to explain. Have you ever met a Cherokee? I met a Cherokee. It was at Harvard Observatory, in the driveway, he was collecting garbage. He said to me, 'I know you! You are Cherokee. I am garbage man now. You are Cherokee.' Then he explained to me that to be a Cherokee you had to believe yourself to be in the centre of the universe. Young children believe the same thing until they discover how vast and uncontrollable the world is, then they presume they must be a what, a

bit player, out on the edge of things. Not so the
Cherokee. Born at the centre of things, he would die at
the centre of things. All true Cherokee believe this. The
Indian I met was a very old man. His sleeve smelled of
ketchup. He told me that once he had understood his
world; his life when a young man had been a prairie
life; he had understood the droughts, the gods, the
buffalo. But all he knew now was his dustcart, a one-
room apartment and a TV to watch. He said he no
longer understood; he was no longer at the centre. No
longer Cherokee. But, he said, he had heard of my head,
of my thoughts like sky; he had seen me on TV. He
said – You are Cherokee! A young colleague of mine
was there. He said not yet, not quite yet had I gotten to
the centre of the universe. He meant I had not yet
unified the fields, finished my work. But, said my proud
colleague to that depressed Indian, just give him
another eighteen months and he'll be slap bang in the
middle. (*Pause.*) I don't want to be at the centre of my
universe, their universe, or anything, of anything at all!

She enters, pristine.

Actress I think you're pathetic. The truth is you don't
give a damn about your work, about people or anything
else. You're so afraid of any upset in your quiet little
life that you let him take away the most precious thing
you ever had. You think it was yours to give away?
Something that valuable isn't yours, it's everyone's. It
was ours and you let it be destroyed! Aren't you
ashamed? The only copy!

Professor The fifth copy.

Actress What?

Professor The fifth.

Actress You have copies?

Professor No. I have destroyed four copies.

Actress I'm not following you.

Professor I have finished my work four times. Each time I have destroyed the calculus and started over. I remember a little more this time than last but there is so much mechanical mathematics I forgot most of what I did before. So I do the work and then I burn the work. Four times now.

Actress But if you studied it, you'd know how it all fits. How the universe works. You'd understand everything!

Professor I am seventy years old. I wouldn't survive the publicity. I want to die quietly where I can just slip off the edge of this dreary, painful world. Like Columbus never did. Unfortunately. What was it your husband said? If Columbus had slipped up we'd all still be Indians. Cherokee.

Actress So you've stopped working?

Professor On the contrary, I keep myself occupied. Mathematics is a splendid waste of time. I get to the end, I forgot the beginning. I go back.

Actress That's awful.

Professor I suppose it is.

Actress It's dreadful! What are you hiding from?

Professor Americans! The God-builders. Listen to them: 'She is the most beautiful, I am this much beautiful; he is the most knowledgeable, I am this much knowledgeable; he is the most powerful, I am hardly powerful at all . . .' They will not take *responsibility* for their world! They want to load it on to others' shoulders, and the weight of all those worlds, I tell you . . .

Actress Look, would you stop talking so goddam smart! I've heard enough. It just sounds like words. I've heard enough words. I want to know you, that's why I came, and you've done nothing but hide behind words. Now what are you hiding from?

Professor Nothing.

Actress Don't lie to me.

Professor Listen . . .

Actress What are you afraid of?

Professor Nothing.

Actress Liar! What are you afraid of? (*Pause.*) Tell me. (*Long pause.*)

Professor There's something . . .

Actress What?

Professor A thought.

Actress Tell me.

Professor No.

Actress Please.

Professor We burned children.

Actress You're not responsible . . .

Professor I am as responsible . . .

Actress No. You don't believe that. Tell me the truth.

Professor (*quietly*) There's something worse.

Actress What could be worse?

Professor I don't know. And I must not think of it.

She puts on her coat, a little of his fear affecting her.

Actress Look, it's over. They won't use those things again. They've said they never will. Besides, figure it out, the people with their fingers on the buttons are the same people who own the stuff that'd get blown to blazes. So they'll never do it. Unless of course they could blow up all the people and leave the buildings standing, which they can't.

The **Professor** *has a thought.*

The **Actress** *feels a little pain. He doesn't notice.*

I have to go. Would you like to hear my lines?

He ignores her. Stands up. There is an enormous explosion. White light hits the windows. The **Professor** *is silhouetted, as is the* **Actress**, *both of them in a wild wind.*

The noise of the explosion stops as suddenly as it started. It was just a thought.

The **Actress** *thumbs her script.*

I take a pot-roast from the oven, I hear the doorbell, I run across the apartment removing my apron, I kiss the man, I disappear. No words. (*She kisses him, or doesn't. She leaves.*)

Unsuitable for Adults

For Mike, with thanks

Unsuitable for Adults was first performed at the Bush Theatre, London, in January 1984. The cast was as follows:

Kate	Felicity Montagu
Harry	Ivor Roberts
Tish	Joanne Pearce
Nick	Tim McInnerny
Keith	Saul Jephcott
Man	Roger Milner

Directed by Mike Bradwell
Décor by Geoff Rose
Lighting by Alan O'Toole
Sound by Annie Hutchinson

Characters

Kate   *Mid twenties, dark, not pretty. Her clothes and manner a little self-consciously unfeminine. Comedian.*

Tish   *Mid twenties, blonde, very pretty, highly strung. Dressed attractively. A stripper.*

Nick   *Late twenties, tall, laconic, good-looking. A talented impersonator.*

Keith   *Late twenties, homely. An untalented magician.*

Harry   *Fifties, a northerner. A brewery publican.*

Man   *Fifties, tall, gaunt.*

Setting

The upstairs room of a pub in Paddington. The room is tall, early Georgian and once quite splendid with painted panels and cornice-work. Now, however, it is in a bad state. It has been decorated three times too often and the huge windows have been tackily blacked out with plywood. Remnants of last year's Christmas decorations are still hanging; a space for a dartboard which has now moved downstairs; redundant posters and notices . . . In one corner a small stage has been built. It is badly lit by a number of small coloured spotlights.

At the end of the play, the scene moves to a lonely stone cottage on Dartmoor. This can either be suggested in the midst of the main setting, or the setting moved out. The latter, if it can be done quickly, is preferable.

Act One

The lights are focused on the little stage. Littered around an empty wooden stool is a girl's school uniform; blazer, blouse, tie, shoes, socks and knickers. A cheap stereo tape deck is visible and plays tacky music suitable for stripping to. A single figure sits looking at the stage, hands deep in the pockets of a combat jacket. The lights change, not very artistically. Enter **Harry**, *collecting glasses.*

Harry Time, gentlemen please! It's gone three o'clock now.

Kate *turns round to look at him. She wears nothing feminine and her hair is cropped, not short, but quite dramatically.*

Time, gentlemen . . . I beg your pardon. Time please, gentlemen and landgirls for the Republic.

Kate *gives him the finger.* **Harry** *goes off with the glasses.* **Kate** *wanders up on to the stage and looks around at the clothing with gentle disdain. She moves towards the centre of the stage and opens her mouth to speak.* **Harry** *returns, ignores her, and reaches across to pick up the knickers. He leaves. Before* **Kate** *can speak again* **Tish** *enters, naked under an old robe or raincoat. She stuffs the school uniform bit by bit into a Sainsbury's carrier bag. She smiles at* **Kate**, *who doesn't smile back, then goes off.* **Kate** *looks out across the room and tries to get the feel of the place. She shudders. As she opens her mouth to speak,* **Tish** *returns.*

Tish Have you seen my knickers?

Kate Yes. I've seen them stretched across your arse, dangling from your index finger, and lying on the floor. I've seen more of your knickers today than I've seen of mine. I should be very surprised if anyone here five minutes ago failed to see your knickers. The entire playground's seen your fucking knickers.

Tish *gives a strange half-cough, half-sneeze.* **Harry** *returns.*

Tish Harry, someone's taken my knickers.

Harry *hands her a fiver.*

Harry Punter made an offer.

Tish Who?

Harry Some bloke.

Tish What bloke? Harry, I wish you wouldn't.

Harry *winks and leaves with more glasses.*

Bet your life he got more than this. I once got offered £25 for a pair of fishnets. I do wish he wouldn't, though. I spend enough of my life in Marks and Spencer's as it is. (**Tish** *turns to leave.*)

Kate You do realise that less than a mile from here, about a week ago, a girl younger than us was raped and had some unnameable object thrust so far into her she died. It was done by a man the *Daily Star* is calling the Son of the Ripper. Had you heard?

A dog barks downstairs.

Tish Yes.

Kate She was his fifth victim. Her name was Angela something.

Tish No, her name was Alison. Excuse me.

The dog barks. **Tish** *leaves.* **Harry** *wanders back.*

Kate Harry, we need more light up here.

Harry Now don't you go touching it. It's electric.

Kate I know it's electric; they're electric lights. That means they're supposed to light up. There they all are, Harry. Wouldn't it be absolutely wonderful if they worked? Wouldn't that be amazing? If what was actually there actually worked?

Harry Bit less of the cheek young lady, and I might find time to have a look this afternoon. Until then don't touch it. (*He shouts through the door to* **Tish**.) Help yourself to a drink, princess. Warm yourself up.

Tish (*off*) Thanks, Harry.

Harry *leaves.* **Tish** *enters and ignores* **Kate**. *She helps herself to a large vodka, sits to drink it, and swallows some antihistamines.*

Kate I was out of order. I apologise. Did you know her?

Tish She was with my agent. She did her first gigs with me; I helped her get her act together. She'd only just left home, but she was very good.

Kate Why do you do it?

Tish Do what? Oh, well, my typing speed's a joke.

Kate I'm serious.

Tish It got me my Equity card.

Kate Christ.

Pause. **Tish** *coughs and sneezes.*

Tish What do you do for a living?

Kate I'm funny.

Tish Oh. I haven't got a sense of humour.

Kate I'm not surprised. (**Kate** *climbs onstage.*)

Tish Are you going to be funny now?

Kate I shouldn't think so. I might be tonight if I manage to get some work done. (*She takes off her* *jacket*.) Christ. What's it like taking all your clothes off in front of two dozen appended penises?

Tish Well, you only put them on to take them off again. It's like you never had them on at all.

Kate But you're a grown woman. Don't you find it humiliating? I find it humiliating enough just watching you.

Harry *has returned for more glasses.*

Harry You leave her alone. It isn't as easy as it looks, her game. There's an art to it. I've seen a lot of them and, believe me, she's good. You know. There's a simplicity in what she does. She's um . . .

Kate Simple.

Harry She's a nice girl. Don't listen to her; you're a nice girl. If I had any daughters left I'd prefer they entered show business than joined the SAS. She's a nice girl. (**Harry** *exits*.)

Kate Which bits are the nicest, Harry?

Tish *coughs*.

I don't care how nice you are. To do what you do you must be pretty desperate or pretty stupid.

Tish I saw a thing on TV about how being funny isn't about being funny at all; it's really about being really, really nasty.

Kate So?

Tish You must be really, really funny.

Kate I'd like to work now, is that OK with you?

Tish Go ahead.

Kate Look, I don't think you'd like the act; would you mind fucking off?

Tish *sneezes*.

Tish Well, I was going to stay. I got a stag this
evening and nowhere to go in between, so Harry said I
could hang around. I don't like to walk the streets
round here at the moment.

Kate Fair enough. (*She steps down from the stage and
turns off the main lights so that the coloured lights remain,
then climbs back.*) Christ.

Tish I can't see your face.

Kate That's because the lights aren't focused on my
face. That's because the lights are focused on someone
else's tits.

Tish *smiles.* **Kate** *gets a chair and climbs on it to reach
the lights.*

Tish Do you know what you're doing?

Kate Of course I don't know what I'm doing. I had to
take four years' fucking cookery. I can make a great
victoria sponge. I'll probably make a bloody great
victoria sponge of this.

Tish Is that a joke?

Kate Yes, that's a joke. Well done. (**Kate** *pulls from the
wall a length of five-by-one with spotlights screwed to it.
She falls off the chair and the lights go out. They are left
in darkness but for a dim glow from somewhere beyond the
serving hatch.*) Oh, bugger.

Tish I don't like the dark.

Kate Very helpful.

Tish Turn the lights on.

Kate I can't turn the lights on. I am bound hand and
foot by the lights.

Tish I'll turn them on then.

Kate Don't you bloody dare.

Tish What shall I do then? Shall I just sit here? What shall I do?

Kate Well, for a start stop acting like a fucking woman.

As they speak, a figure rises from behind the hatch. It is a tall figure with a strange, shiny bald head. **Kate** *sees it, though it remains behind* **Tish.**

Who's there?

Tish Me.

Kate Who is it?

Tish Me. I'm here.

Kate Shut up.

Tish Why?

The figure very slowly begins to climb over the bar.

Kate Come here.

Tish Where?

Kate Come over here.

Tish I can't see anything.

Kate Just get up and come here.

Tish Why?

Kate Because there's some fucker behind you!!

Tish *turns and screams. She runs across the room overturning a few chairs. The figure picks up a meat cleaver, then disappears from the light. After a few seconds' silence, the main lights come on. Standing by the light switch is a tall man wearing a plastic bald head and glasses. He looks around him, blinking like an owl. It is* **Nick,** *doing a remarkably good impersonation of Eric Morecambe.*

Nick (*Morecambe*) I'm sorry about that.

Kate You bastard.

Nick Is that you, Ern? That is fantastic. Your own mother wouldn't know you. What are you, a Christmas tree?

Kate Insensitive little shit!

Nick Can she say that?

Kate You frightened the life out of her. Why do you do things like that:

Nick (*Brando*) The horror. Because of the horror. The look of horror on your face . . .

Kate Nick!

Nick (*turns the bald head around and becomes Kojak*) Who loves you, baby? Daddy does. Stavros! Lock these broads away and don't let anybody get at them! (**Nick** *exits.*)

Kate Are you OK?

Tish *nods and rises in a slight state of shock. She takes an asthma spray from her bag and uses it.*

I'm sorry. He thinks he's funny. What's wrong?

Tish Nothing. I'm always like this. I have to go to the loo.

Tish *leaves.* **Kates** *prepares to work.* **Nick** *walks in on his knees doing ET.*

Nick Elliot, I go home. (*ET picks his nose.*) Gift for Elliot. (*Elliot.*) Oh boy, he's a cute little fella. I'll keep him as a pet. What do I call him? (*ET.*) Call him HIV.

Kate Do you get *all* your material off toilet walls?

Nick (*James Stewart*) Katherine, welcome home. I've missed you so damned awfully I could cry. I'm sorry to get emotional. It's just that I love you, Katherine.

Kate Well, you've got a fucking evil way of showing it.

He kisses her.

Don't.

Nick (*De Niro*) Oh come on, hey, what's one little kiss? Kiss gonna kill you?

Kate Look, I've had time to think and I don't want to get involved again, OK? I don't want my miserable little life entwined with your miserable little life. Or anyone's. It sounds like a cliché, I know, but since I've been away I've learned to be alone and it's the best thing I ever taught myself.

Nick (*Tom Conti*) It's hard to explain, this being in love. Trying to explain what being in love is like is like trying to explain Day-Glo orange to someone who went blind the week before they invented it. It's so orange you can't imagine, you tell him. I've seen orange, he says. But this is more orange than that, you tell him. Like a Belisha beacon, he says. Like the fruit, orange? No, you say, more orange than orange. That's how I love you.

Kate Who the fuck was that?

Nick Tom Conti.

Kate Nick, that's a bit obscure.

Nick Yes, but he's very good at sincerity. (*He kisses her.*)

Kate And who was that?

Nick Who would you like?

Kate Oh no . . .

Nick Anyone you want, Katey.

Kate Bastard. (*Pause.*) Robert De Niro.

Nick No problem. (*He does a lot of preparation, then kisses her like Robert De Niro.*)

Kate Not bad. Sean Connery.

Nick *thinks for a moment.*

Nick (*Sean Connery*) OK, let me see now, I've always had a penchant for kissing pussy galore, so if you'd just take your clothes off, Miss Moneypenny . . .

Kate Nick, that's not funny.

He kisses her again, unhurriedly.

Kate Mmm hmm. Richard Pryor.

Nick Then get your ass over here, motherfucker. Or I'll get my ass over there. (*He kisses her again.*) Macho-man! I put your tongue right down your throat, I'm Macho-man.

Kate Mick Jagger.

Nick You old slag. (*He kisses her.*)

Kate Thank you. No, that's quite enough.

Nick Nastassia Kinski.

Kate You'll be lucky.

Nick My turn! Nastassia Kinski.

Kate It's your game, not mine.

Nick Oh, don't be bloody mean. Give us um . . . Isabelle Huppert.

Kate Get off, you lecherous sod. (*She kisses him anyway.*)

Nick Who was that?

Kate Me.

Nick Oh wow. Big deal.

She thumps him.

Nick Your turn.

Kate You.

They look at each other.

You.

Nick ET.

Kate No, never!

They struggle. He pins her down.

Nick Bob Monkhouse.

Kate Get off me.

Nick Rowan Atkinson.

Kate Fucking get off me!!

He gets off her.

Nick Prince Charles?

Kate You.

Nick Michael Caine.

Kate I want you. That's all, I just want you.

Nick John Hurt.

Kate John Hurt?

Nick John Hurt.

Kate OK.

Nick John Hurt in *The Elephant Man*.

Kate No!

She screams. They fight. The fight turns into a clinch and the clinch into a kiss. They cuddle up to each other.

Who's this? Is this you? I don't trust you. Not one little bit.

(**Tish** *returns, looking great.*)

Tish Sorry.

Nick (*Cliff*) Hi.

Tish Hello.

Kate This is Nick. This is . . .

Tish Tish. Um . . . (*Sneezes.*)

Nick Pleased to meet you. Hi.

Tish Hello.

They look at each other.

Kate Oh shit.

Nick You what?

Kate I'd just like to say that if you two ever go to bed together I'll hang myself in both your bathrooms.

Nick Oh, come on, Kate . . .

Tish Honestly.

Nick *and* **Tish** *look at each other for half a second longer than is diplomatic.* **Nick** *looks at* **Kate** *as* **Tish** *looks away.* **Tish** *looks at* **Kate** *as* **Nick** *looks away.*

Kate Second thoughts, I'll do it straight away.

Nick Kate, we've only just met. You just introduced us.

Kate I know. I just don't like to feel I'm standing in anybody's way, that's all.

Nick Katey, you're completely bloody paranoid.

Kate I am not paranoid! I am genuinely hated by a great many people. I am regularly done in, shat on and betrayed by my closest friends. If I'm paranoid, Mrs Tebbit's a hypochondriac!

Enter **Harry**.

Harry (*to* **Nick**) Right, I've got some bones to pick with you. First, I've had to get in another barman because young Jane won't serve up here no more. She had to say three Hail Marys last week after watching you lot. So I've got an extra man on and you're paying for him.

Nick Oh, come on, Harry, you know how much we take.

Harry I'll go a third.

Nick Fifty-fifty.

Harry All right, fifty-fifty. But I want another interval.

Nick Harry, if we have another interval there'll be more intervals than acts.

Harry You know what's wrong with the New Left? Half the buggers drink St Clements and the other half are under the table after one bottle of Pils. If it wasn't for Pernod I'd go bust. Get some beer drinkers in, will you, or I'll cancel you and book in the Women-Only Disco. None of them'd be seen dead with a half-pint glass.

Nick (*Harry*) All right, Harry. I'll do my best to get them pissed and legless . . .

Harry Oh aye, very clever.

Nick Oh aye.

Harry Oh aye.

Nick Very clever.

Harry Oh, and there's a message for you. Some bloke called from Cardiff. Sounded like a coloured chap.

Nick What'd he say?

Harry He said he left his bookings diary at Scotch Corner and was it tonight?

Nick Yes, it's tonight.

Harry How many of them?

Nick Don't worry, Harry; they're a bit like the Black and White Minstrels.

Harry I don't care what colour they are as long as there's no bloody oildrums! You're to phone him anyway if he's coming. Fifteen-piece bloody brass bands . . . (*Exit* **Harry**.)

Kate Who are they?

Nick Bunch of Rastas I saw in Edinburgh.

Kate Coming from Cardiff?

Nick Yes. Local band. Ja Cymru. (**Nick** *leaves, having found his address book.*)

Tish Are you and Nick um . . .

Kate I think the word's entwined.

Tish But you do have a relationship?

Kate I wouldn't say that. Trying to make a relationship of what we have is a bit like trying to decorate a trifle after you've thrown it against the wall.

Tish I see.

Kate I'm sorry if I was a little premature there, but you're definitely his type.

Tish How do you mean?

Kate You're female. I mean, look at you. I can't compete with that. He'll want you, and he usually gets what he wants. It's inevitable.

Tish Well, perhaps I'll say no.

Kate Yeah. Look, I haven't done a gig in two months; do you mind if I get on with some work?

Tish What is it you do exactly?

Kate I told you. I'm funny. I'm very funny, or at least I was.

Tish Why was?

Kate I haven't been around for a while. I don't know if I feel funny any more.

Tish Why not?

Kate Well, there are a lot of things in this world that drive me up the wall. I thought if I made fun of them they wouldn't but as it turned out they now drive me up the wall and across the ceiling.

Tish What things?

Kate Oh, men in particular. Men in general. Men in TR7s. Men in Jiffy T-shirts. You name it. If I want it, it doesn't want me. If it wants me it's a garden gnome. I've never had a man who didn't do me in.

Tish Neither have I.

Kate I got off to a terrible start. I lost my virginity to a Spaniard.

Tish So did I. So did I.

Kate I was fourteen.

Tish That's amazing. So was I.

Kate I was raped.

Tish Oh, I'm sorry.

Kate You needn't be. He was only twelve, and I was on top. It happened, to my eternal shame, in a hotel in Marbella. Where did you find yours?

Tish School cruise. Five of us decided we'd all lose our virginity by the time we reached Athens. The others all had spotty third formers from Ampleforth. I did much better. I had our waiter. His name was Jaquemo.

Kate Sounds painfully exotic.

Tish Well, Daddy was in the Diplomatic so I had my

ear nibbled in every country under the sun, when I
was younger. I've made love on a beach in Oman, on a
night train through Germany, in a shack on stilts in
Singapore. You name it. It's not that I'm romantic, I'm
just susceptible to environments. I find it awfully hard
to say no. I think I've only said no once and that was to
Colin Welland. At least he said he was Colin Welland.

Kate Colin Welland?

Tish Well, he looked like Colin Welland. That's why I
said no. Anyway, he wasn't, he was just this bloke who
told everyone he was.

Kate Jesus. I hate men. No wonder my sex life is
awful; I loathe the bastards. Especially the ones that
come up to you and say 'Hello'. I can't stand it when a
man comes up to me and says it like that. 'Hello.'

Enter **Keith**, *carrying part of a public address system. He
puts it down and smiles.*

Keith Hi.

Kate Close enough.

Keith *does a trick. It's quite a good one and* **Tish** *quite
enjoys it.* **Kate** *is not in the least impressed.*

Tish Oh wow, that's amazing. That's really good.

Kate Very, very boring.

Keith Have I shown you it before?

Kate No, it was boring the first time.

Tish How do you do it?

Keith Ahah!

Kate For Christ's sake, Keith, tell her how it's done.

Keith It's magic.

Kate What are you doing here anyway? We don't start
until nine. I want to rehearse, Keith. I haven't done a

gig in two months and everyone and his dog's here. You've got bloody awful timing and I wish you'd all just fuck off. Hello.

Keith How are you?

Kate Fine.

Keith How's Pattie?

Kate In Brighton.

Keith Good to see you.

Kate Thank you.

Pause.

Keith Do you know anything about this guy from Channel Four? Supposed to be a guy from Channel Four coming in tonight.

Kate Oh yes? Well, if they'd only get themselves organised we could do them a party booking.

Keith Well, you never know, do you? (*Exit* **Keith**.)

Kate That's Keith.

Tish A magician.

Kate I wouldn't go that far. Nick only put him on the bill because he owns a crappy PA.

Tish He seems nice.

Kate He's very nice. And he's a dickhead.

Tish I know what you mean. It's easy to like them when they're harmless, isn't it?

They both laugh.

Kate Will you stay and watch the show tonight?

Tish I've got shows myself tonight.

Kate Well, when I run through, then. Will you listen?

Tish Why?

Kate Why not?

Tish Why me?

Kate I want to see if I can make you laugh.

Tish No, you don't. You want to see if you can make me think because you think I don't.

Kate *laughs.*

Kate Fair enough.

Harry *backs through the door carrying a toolbox. He finds the lights on the floor.*

Harry Oh, no problem. I see you fixed them.

Kate Ha ha. Can I use the downstairs bar to work?

Harry What's wrong with the next room?

Kate Nothing Rentokil couldn't deal with.

Harry You've made a right bloody mess of this.

Kate *goes.*

I'll need my other box. Are you all right, princess?

Tish Mmm? Yes.

Harry Good. You want to watch her, you know. I reckon, don't you?

He winks at her and leaves. **Tish** *sighs a huge sigh and then sneezes.* **Nick** *enters and she jumps.*

Nick (*Bogart*) How are you doing, angel? My name's Nick.

Tish I know your name.

Nick (*Cary Grant*) You're looking a little depressed. I thought being a man of great personality and style I might be able to cheer you up somewhat.

Tish Who's that?

Nick Judy, Judy, Judy . . .

Tish I don't know. I can't tell half of them.

Nick (*John Wayne*) You want I should make it simple for you, pilgrim.

Tish Clint Eastwood?

Nick No.

Tish Well, who cares, anyway. I don't. I just want . . .

Nick (*Basil Fawlty*) Yes?! What?!

Tish A chat.

Nick A cat?! Manuel!! Would you like roast cat? Or fried cat? Or maybe a cold cat salad? (*Manuel.*) Hyes, Mista Hfwalty? (*Basil.*) Manuel, serve this lady, will you? She seems to want to eat a cat! (*Manuel.*) Que? (*Basil.*) No, a cat. She wants a cat! (*Manuel.*) Oh! A chat. Talky talky. (*Basil.*) Yes, I might have guessed you'd understand each other.

Tish Why won't you let me kiss you any more?

Nick (*Jack Nicholson*) Well Doc, I guess it's because the next woman I kiss is gonna light up like a goddam Christmas tree.

Tish Nick . . .

Nick Look.

Tish What?

Nick Kate's back. I don't want to hurt her.

Tish Why not?

Nick (*Kenneth Williams*) Because she'd hurt me back. (*Sid James.*) With a machete.

Tish I wish you'd said.

Nick If I'd said then we wouldn't know each other as well as we do now and I think that would be a shame, don't you?

Tish (*sneezes*) I don't know you at all.

Nick Well, I'm nothing special, am I?

Tish (*wipes her nose*) You made me laugh.

Nick Well . . . that's my job.

Tish You lied to me.

Nick I said exactly what I felt.

Tish If you don't feel it afterwards I think that's lying.

Nick Well, if I've changed my mind it's not, is it? Be rational for Christ's sake.

Keith *enters with the rest of the PA.*

Keith Hi, Nick, how's it going?

Nick (*Keith*) Hi, Keith, things are great with me, how are things with you?

Keith You bastard.

Nick (*Keith*) You bastard.

Keith Is there anyone you can't do?

Nick Richard Gere. I mean you've got to have something to start with, right?

Keith Do you know anything about this Channel Four guy coming in?

Nick Yeah, apparently he's been sent on a mission to find out what happened to the others.

Keith Oh well, you never know.

Keith *sets up the PA.* **Nick** *and* **Tish** *talk quietly.*

Nick Look, I wanted you and I told you I wanted you, that's all.

Tish It was the way you told me.

Nick (*Coward*) Very eloquently if I remember rightly.
I'm very sorry; I'll give myself a handicap next time.
I'll only use phrases like, 'You have lovely eyes; suck
this.'

Tish I'd prefer that to all the rubbish you talked about
living for the moment.

Nick Look, I never lied. I made no promises.

Tish Yes, you did, whatever you did or didn't say to
me you made love to me, and that's a promise.

Nick Oh, come on . . .

Tish And you've broken it. You know you have.

Nick *moves away.*

Nick (*to* **Keith**) Have you fixed this pile of crap?

Keith Yes, it was only I'd left the spare fuse at home.

Nick Have you got it with you this week?

Keith Oh yeah. It's in the amp. Actually, Nick, I've
been thinking and I think I need two spots really. I
think I need one early on for the escapology and one
later on for the magic proper, what do you think?

Nick Take it from me, Keith, they'd never let you on
twice.

Keith Nick, do you like my act? No, be honest.

Nick (*Alexei Sayle*) Well, to be honest, if it's honesty
you want, I'm not exactly in love with you, no. As a
matter of fact I only ever wanted you for your PA. I
mean you've got a great pair of Ohms, you know what I
mean?

(*He glances at* **Tish** *and leaves.* **Tish** *and* **Keith** *look at
each other, embarrassed. Neither can think of anything to
say.* **Keith** *is just about to resort to a trick when* **Harry**

*comes in. He carries a hammer and the evening paper
which he throws down on to the table. Beneath the
headline 'Face of a Killer?' is an identikit picture of a
gaunt man in his late fifties.*)

Harry Here he is, then. Artist's impression. I'm not a
vindictive man but personally I'd cut his bollocks off.
You walk down the street nowadays and a nice pretty
girl walks towards you and you look at her legs, you
know. It's natural. Or you look at what she's wearing or
at her face . . . and then you see it in her eyes. She
doesn't trust you. You've never met her, you're never
likely to, but you've looked. So as she passes you there's
this wave of fear; you can feel it. He's got a lot to
bloody answer for. You used to be able to smile at a
pretty girl.

Keith I think the problem is, Harry, this socket
definitely gets overloaded. I've got an extension cable in
my Dad's boot; if you've got a two-way adaptor we
could bring some wattage in from the next room
without blowing the jukebox this time, what do you
think?

Harry I think if you don't get into your heads this is
not the London Palladium somebody's going to die up
here.

Keith I'll get the extension. It'll be safer in the long
run.

Keith *goes.* **Harry** *begins to repair the lights.*

Harry I'm sorry about your underthings. I thought
this time of the year you could do with a little extra
cash.

Tish This time of the year I could do with a little
extra clothing.

Harry Are you going home for Christmas?

Tish Oh, I wouldn't be very welcome.

Harry I think you should go home. What with this business . . .

Tish It's all right.

Harry It's a nasty business.

Tish I'll be all right.

Harry You better be careful.

Tish Please, look, I'll be all right.

Harry You should go home. Your parents would be pleased to see you.

Tish My parents aren't exactly proud of me.

Harry Do they know where you are?

Tish Not exactly.

Harry I suppose what it is is they don't understand you, right?

Tish No, they just don't like me. My mother and I only have one thing in common and we both hate him. All the women I've ever known hate men.

Harry I've had two wives and three daughters. I drove one to her grave, one to the bottle and the other three out of the house. I am single-handedly to blame for wrecking the lives of five different women and personally responsible for 4000 years of male domination. Or so I used to be told. There you are. Three daughters. (*He shows* **Tish** *a couple of photographs.*)

Tish What are their names?

Harry Regan, Goneril and Lucretia. That's Jennifer, that's Tracey, and that's Paula. She's in California. Tracey's disappeared and Jenny married a man called Gavin. You know the type; would never tell you what his job was but drove a BMW and anything you mentioned could get it for you cheap. She weren't exactly a beauty were Jenny. A lot older than the other two. Paula was always the bright one, and Tracey the pretty one. Jenny took them both in hand when their mother went off to the clinic. She was a good kid, but boring, you know what I mean? Anyway, I'd said to Paula, you're a bright girl, you've got a quick mind, I'm buggered if you're going to waste it. If it costs me a small fortune you're going to secretarial school. And Tracey I thought'd make a good model, you know. Classy stuff like. Or if it turned out she could sing she'd be a damn sight better than some you see on the box; I'd do my best to get her on one of those discovery shows, you know. But Jenny, well, to be quite honest, I don't know what Gavin saw in her. Except she had a sweet nature, of course. What I mean is, I'm surprised that meant bugger all to Gavin. Anyway, they got wed. Tracey was bridesmaid. Paula on the other hand announced that she didn't believe in marriage or any other form of social oppression and refused to come to the ceremony. I said to her, you're a selfish little cow and if you won't come to your own sister's wedding you can leave this house. I bloody will, she said. So I gave her a backhander and she bloody did. Anyway, Jenny got wed on a wet Thursday down the Paddington registry and we came back here to celebrate. I didn't feel much like celebrating; I had to give this Gavin my own tie two minutes before the ceremony. He seemed to think he was nipping in to back a horse. But my thinking was Jenny's mother'd feel bad enough there was no church service; she'd spin in her bloody grave if there was no reception either. Our people made a good show considering; dozen of them came down in a minibus. Pissed out of their brains before they got here. His side of the family was a right shambles, though; some batty old aunt who'd read about it in the local paper and a couple of bloody wide-boy mates of his with their so-called girlfriends. I'd put two hundred quid in the till; soon as that ran out they buggered off. Our lot enjoyed themselves though, it would have been a good night.

Tish What happened?

Harry Oh, there was a run on Scotch so I came up here to get some more. Gavin was up here. Jenny, bless her heart, was downstairs knee-deep in non-stick frying pans and Gavin's up here with our Tracey. They were on that table, at least she was, with her blue satin frock up round her waist. I felt sick. I said to her, 'That's it. You're out. I'm finished with you.' 'He made me,' she said. 'He made me.' Did he, buggery. I gave her the back of my hand. I hadn't hit that girl for years. And this Gavin, this son-in-law of mine, didn't lift a bloody finger. He just watched.

Tish Didn't you hit him?

Harry He weren't worth the trouble. I went downstairs and told Jenny. I was buggered if I was going to leave her in ignorance. His car was outside; his mates had covered it in shaving cream. Jenny were sat in a corner. He came down and just started drinking again. They were going to drive down to Brighton for the night, so eventually Jenny got up and she took him round the bar into the parlour. It was noisy in here but I could hear them arguing. Jenny had a mouth on her at times. Then I heard her hit the floor. I was in there like lightning; he'd hit her. I said, you evil bastard, get out of my pub. I'd have had him that time if my brother Charlie hadn't held me off. But suddenly Jenny's shouting, 'Look, go away . . . go away and leave us alone!' And Charlie dragged me out. Ten minutes later I looked back in and there they are. He's on the floor with her, and she's cradling his head in her arms. And this hand of his is on her knee, with a flashy gold ring on it, and Jenny's ear bleeding where it caught her. Like babes in the bloody wood. So I said, 'If you go with him, you go for ever.' She went. So . . . Jenny's married to a man who'll bring her nowt but misery; Paula's in California; and Tracey, I've no idea. So don't ask me about women. Every woman I've known it always got to the point where all I could do was ignore them or thump them. In the end it always seemed best to part company.

Tish I don't think you understand women much.

Harry That's what they tell me. All my life women have told me I don't understand women. Well, you're wrong. Tell you the truth, the only thing I don't understand about women is what the bloody hell they see in us.

(**Harry** *completes his work.* **Kate** *enters, followed by* **Nick**.)

Kate Right, I don't care if you stay or piss off. I want to use the stage. Keith! I'm getting nervous about this. Christ, the last gig I did was a Tuesday night in Chiswick.

Enter **Keith**.

Keith What?

Kate Sit.

Keith *sits, as do the others.* **Kate** *changes the lights.*

Kate (*to* **Nick**) Will you tell me if this is funny? I really need to know.

Nick (*Bilko*) How many times do I have to tell you? You're funny, funny, funny. All right, snap to it; let's hear the funny material!

Kate *takes off her sweater and as she drops it goes into a brief reverie. She snaps herself out of it quickly.*

Kate Well, introduce me then.

Nick OK, OK. (*Prince Charles.*) Er, ladies and gentlemen, er, my wife Diana, who unfortunately can't be with us tonight as she's home getting pregnant, has called our next act the best entertainment she's had since Sardines at Balmoral when Andrew showed her all the secret passages she never knew were there . . .

Kate Nick!

Nick Now then, now then, now then, sensation seekers, guys and gals, what do we have? We have for you, live and alone on stage, as it happens, a charming feminist with fabulous tits . . .

Kate Get on with it.

Nick Ladies and gentlemen . . . Kate Kelvin!! How about that then?

Kate *strides into the spotlight.*

Kate Hello, goodevening. My name's Kate Kelvin and as God's gift just pointed out, I am a woman, and I do have breasts. In fact the reason women have breasts, you may never have been told the actual biological reason, but the reason women have breasts is so that men will talk to them. Men are very interested in women. They are. I had a man make love to me just the other week. And while he was at it I moved. And he said, sorry darling, did I hurt you? I said, no, no, I was just turning the page of my magazine.

But seriously, I'm here to tell you what the problem is for women. The problem for women in general, and female comedians in particular, but generally the problem for women is that they can't piss in public and maintain their dignity at the same time. For men, pissing in public is probably the most dignified thing they can do, you know? (*She imitates some very cocky public pissing.*) But women. Forget it. It's all nettle stings and weeing in your knickers, right? And it's a big problem for me, especially. Lenny Bruce, he came to England thirty years ago and he took a slash on the drapes and he became famous. He became a hero. Can you imagine what a prick I'd look?

I can see we've got a critic here; he wrote down the reference to Lenny Bruce. You going to mention Lenny Bruce in a column about me? I'm very flattered. I'm deeply, deeply flattered. He's going to look down and piss all over you, but I'm deeply flattered. Lenny Bruce was OK in my books. As racist, sexist, Jewish men go, he was OK.

Nick He was a fuck sight better than you!

Pause.

I'm heckling. I'm heckling.

Kate All right. All right. What did you say?

Nick I said Bruce was a better comedian than you are.

Kate Yes, well I'm a better fuck. No, that's dreadful.

Nick Go for the throat.

Kate OK. OK. That's a very nice suit you're wearing, sir. I hear they're very fashionable. Again.

Nick Heard it before. Very boring.

Kate Look, I'm trying to concentrate, so just shut the fuck up.

Nick Oh, very witty.

Kate Shut up! Let's discuss this later; perhaps at your parents' wedding. For the moment I'm talking and I'd like to talk about fucking.

I like to talk about fucking because thanks to the kind of men I meet I find talking about it much more stimulating than doing it most of the time. Don't get me wrong; I'm not frigid. There are times I'll fuck anything, so long as it's vegetable or mineral. You know what I mean? Did you ever have one of those weekends on your own when you just can't stop? I do. I have fucked everything in our house. You name it, it has given me pleasure. I mean, after all, it's more enjoyable with inanimate objects. You don't have to tell a shower hose you thought he was great. And you don't have to make coffee for them and you don't have to make funny little squeaking noises for them either.

'Oooohoh . . .!' There's no pretence. You don't have to pretend bugger-all for a shampoo bottle. If it's not doing anything for you you don't have to encourage it, you just put it back on the shelf. Shampoo won't give a shit. It's not going to give you the third degree, you know?

'I know you're fucking something else, don't ask me how, I can just feel it in my deep-down cleanser. Who are you fucking?'

'No one. Nothing. Don't get yourself in a lather.'

'Don't lie to me.'

'All right. All right. I admit it. I fucked the telephone.'

'The telephone? How could you fuck the telephone?'

'Look, I fucked it once. Once. I was drunk and it just happened, that's all.'

'What's the telephone do for you that I can't do for you?'

'The telephone talks to me. You never talk to me.'

'I'm a shampoo bottle; I'm not good with words. Who else have you been with?'

'No one else.'

'Who else?'

'OK. You know that little appliance for doing the corners on the stairs that fits into the vacuum cleaner . . .? We had a thing together. But it was before I even bought you.'

'You never really loved me at all, did you?'

'Look, I like you. I'll always like you. You're good for my hair; I get a really nice shine with you, but you just don't turn me on any more.'

'You're a real bitch. Try washing your hair with the

telephone or the vacuum cleaner; see how well they treat you. And let me tell you something for your own good: that little appliance for doing the stairs, there's nowhere he hasn't poked himself . . .'

You get none of that. The nice boy in the front row is looking a little confused. That was a routine about masturbation. We do it too but we don't go blind. We don't even close our eyes.

Of course, masturbation is very popular nowadays, because it's safe. Everyone's decided that sex had better be safe. Surprised me, because I'd always thought that safe sex was infinitely preferable to any other type. I don't think many women have ever liked dangerous sex, but apparently it takes a killer disease to get men thinking along those lines. But I feel sorry for men actually.

I mean, it must be very different now for men. When the girl leans forwards in her purple satin blouse: He Knows the Risks.

And when she plucks at her sheer black tights with her polished fingernails: The Choice is His. He knows that after they've joined Rupert Bear on the bed, she'll have given him Aids.

And if she hasn't given him Aids it won't be long before she's stabbing him in the chest with a bread knife.

It's his own fault. He shouldn't have gotten so nervous in the restaurant. Shouldn't have tried to light her cigarette with that packet of condoms. But she smiled . . .

'Oh, how thoughtful. Only our first date and he's brought a packet of Rainbow Jiffis with him. What a nice man.'

Obviously all right to fuck *him* then, isn't it?

Cheeky sod. Time was at the end of a posh meal you used to get an After Eight mint, not a Durex Featherlite.

Still, we women have always enjoyed passing on diseases, haven't we? Soon as I heard about Aids I rushed out and slept with a lot of gay men so that I could pass it on to all those unsuspecting hetero males.

It must be very confusing for the lads though, mustn't it? To Be Prepared or not to Be Prepared. A whole generation of girls laid end to end for the boys by the hippie revolution and *Cosmo* magazine and suddenly they're all pulling up their knickers and using words like love and faithfulness . . . Free love's dead then. Monogamy's back. Big joke.

That's it. That's the new stuff. (**Kate** *turns the lights back on.*)

Harry That your idea of humour, is it?

Kate Yes.

Harry Not funny though, is it?

Kate No, it isn't really. (**Kate** *corners* **Nick.**) Well? Do you think it's funny? Do you think I'm funny?

Nick No, but you are a great fuck.

Harry Hey, language! (**Harry** *exits.*)

Kate Thanks, that's very encouraging.

Keith I thought it was fantastic. Really. Fantastic.

Kate Fuck off.

Keith *fiddles with his PA.*

Nick?

Nick Derivative. It's not you up there yet, it's Richard Pryor with PMT.

Keith Actually, I've been thinking. I think I'll trade in these Ohms and get a couple of Bose. I mean it's only money, isn't it? What do you think?

Nick How about another mike?

Keith How about another spot?

Nick How about getting off my back?

Kate What shall I do then? What shall I do?

Nick Just be you, right?

Nick *leaves,* **Keith** *follows him.*

Keith It's no big deal, it's just I get them warmed up and then I'm off, you know . . .

He leaves. **Kate** *sits at* **Tish**'*s table.*

Kate Well?

Tish Oh, it was lovely. It was really good.

Kate You hated it.

Tish No, really, it was . . .

Kate Dreadful.

Tish No, well . . . it wasn't really what . . .

Kate What did you hate about it?

Tish Well, I don't know, but I suppose . . . Look, I liked it.

Kate You're a little liar! What did you bloody well think?

Tish Well, I found it a bit offensive actually.

Kate Oh, you found it offensive?

Tish I don't know. A bit.

Kate You found it obscene?

Tish Well, no . . .

Kate That which offends is obscene.

Tish All right then, I don't know. Obscene.

Kate As in pornographic?

Tish I don't know.

Kate It's the same thing!

Tish Is it?

Kate Yes.

Tish All right then, it was pornographic.

Kate *gets up.*

Kate Then I don't know why I bother. I should leave it to you, I suppose. You're obviously the more entertaining of the two of us.

Tish No. You were very good. It's just I didn't really understand the jokes.

Kate The jokes aren't the point. You're meant to listen to what I'm saying. Did you hear a thing I said?

Tish I don't know. I was waiting for a joke.

Enter **Nick.**

Nick The call box is knackered. I've got to go home and call these bloody Welshmen. Do you want a cup of coffee?

Kate Yeah, OK. I'll get my coat. (**Kate** *leaves.*)

Nick Look, I'd like to see you again but Kate and I have got this thing . . . you know how things are.

Tish She's going to hate me, isn't she? First she'll hate us both, then she'll love you again and just hate me. That's not fair.

Nick She's not going to hate you because she's not going to know. Look, there's no reason we can't be friends.

Kate *returns. Exit* **Nick**. **Kate** *calls* **Tish**'s *attention to the newspaper lying on the table.*

Kate I'm sorry, but you said you knew her. Don't you understand why she died? Because she was available. Because women like you make yourselves available. They're killing us now for sport. One man rips us up so the rest of them can read about it; get a little pang of feeling in their cocks under the breakfast table. It's a thirst. And you think I perform pornography?

Tish I never said that.

Kate That's the trouble! You've got nothing to say. You've got to work out what you hate about this shitty place and then do something about it. And the first thing to do is break silence. Say what you think. Say something.

Tish Umm . . .

Kate Well then do something. For her at least. Something.

Exit **Kate**. *Enter* **Harry**.

Harry I have to go now; couple of frames. I'll have to lock up the place around you as usual. You be all right until five-thirty?

Tish Yes.

Harry Don't drink too much.

Tish Yes.

Harry Be good, princess.

Tish Harry?

Harry Yes?

Tish What do you think when you watch me work? Do you ever get any funny ideas? You know?

Harry Me? No. Not guilty.

He looks at her and then leaves. **Tish** *listens as the doors below are slammed and locked. The dog barks, then there is quiet. Over a long period,* **Tish** *becomes jumpy and frightened. This causes her to sneeze and scratch and makes her breathing more and more difficult. Upset with herself, she takes out some tablets to help her sneezing. Slowly she makes a little collection of bottles on the table of everything from aspirin to Haliborange. She pours herself a large vodka and a glass of water and returns to her table. She begins slowly to take the tablets. We watch her move into a slow routine of swallowing. We watch her take at least three dozen tablets.*

The lights fade.

Act Two

The same. **Tish**'s *eyes are closed. Her head nods and jerks a few times. When she finally falls asleep her head hits the table with a bang and she wakes. She sees the jars and bottles in front of her as if for the first time. Like a naughty child she hides the mess by sweeping it into her bag. The moment of panic gives way to her tiredness and she begins to nod off again, but there is fear now. The dog barks loudly downstairs. The darker it becomes for her, the less she wants it to grow dark.* **Keith** *enters.*

Keith Hi. Have you got a minute? Can I show you something? It's one I haven't tried yet.

Tish *can't fathom what's happening. She just stares at him.*

You look knackered. Are you OK?

Pause. **Tish** *sighs and looks confused.*

Sorry, were you asleep? I'm sorry, I'll go away.

Keith *turns to go.* **Tish** *discovers an empty bottle in her hand, remembers what she's done, and jumps up to stop him. She's afraid, but too far gone to speak. Another impasse.*

I used to just do it for fun as a kid but I thought, well, why not give it a go? It's still very popular, magic. Vavoom! (*He does an impression of Tommy Cooper that almost makes her fall over.*) Sorry.

He turns to go again. **Tish** *grabs him and pushes him into the middle of the room, then sits herself on a chair in front of him. She has difficulty focusing but convinces him she wants to watch.*

Right, um . . . OK. This is a new thing I've been
working on, so don't watch too carefully. (*Pause.*) Er,
I'm not quite ready; could you close your eyes for a
moment?

Tish *shakes her head as it is an unwise suggestion.*

It's not cheating; there's always some preparation. It's
just that I don't have a leggy assistant to make you look
over there. (*He points. She looks.*) No, I mean, er . . .
Could you just cover your eyes up for a second?

*She covers her eyes. He pops a billiard ball into his mouth.
This makes it impossible for him to tell her to open her
eyes. He removes the ball.*

OK, you can open them now.

*She opens and focuses. This makes it impossible for him to
return the ball to his mouth.*

Sorry, look, could you just close them again and er,
count to five and open them? Sorry.

*She closes her eyes. He puts the ball in his mouth. He
stands like a magician and waits. And waits. She doesn't
open her eyes because she has fallen asleep. Eventually he
removes the ball.*

OK.

And pops it back in again quickly. **Tish** *doesn't respond,
so eventually he taps her on the shoulder. She rouses and
focuses once more. He smiles and stands like a magician.
As he is about to start the trick . . .*

Tish What's your name again?

*He is banjaxed once more. He coughs a quick ingenious
cough and spits out the ball into his hand, where he palms
it.*

Keith My name's Keith. I know, I know. But I find it
works to my advantage, like a boy named Sue, you
know?

Tish *feels herself drowsing.*

Tish Keith?

Keith Are you sure you're all right?

Tish Would you show me this trick, please?

Keith Sure. OK. Er . . . What's that up there?

He points in the air to misdirect her. She stares at him steadfastly.

Up there!

She still stares straight at him.

You're making this very difficult, you realise that.

Suddenly he dashes around her, putting the ball in his mouth on the way round. She loses him entirely for a moment, then focuses on him again. He stands like a magician, she sits like a rabbit in headlights. He does the trick, producing half a dozen balls from his mouth, a few from his ears, multiplying and vanishing them, finally producing a ball from her ear, a lemon from his own, and a grapefruit from God knows where. **Tish** *is the best audience he's ever had. She remains glued to every move, and when the trick is over, she stays glued.*

Da-da! I thank you.

She can't respond yet.

I really think you could do with some sleep. Why don't you get your head down . . .

Tish No, please . . .

Keith Oh no, I'm sorry. I never tell anyone how they're done. It's magic.

Keith *leaves.* **Tish** *gets up, goes behind the bar, and throws up. From below the sound of doors being unlocked.* **Tish** *sits down and composes herself.* **Kate** *enters, followed by* **Nick.**

Nick (*Richard Burton*) It's very easy really. You see, you put your lips together and pop some air out and you get a puh, or a buh, or you can use your tongue and get a duh or a cuh or a guh and then if you keep your mouth open and change the shape of your lips about you can get vowels like eee or aaa or ooo; listen to me Elizabeth and then you put them all together: puh, duh, guh, eee, aaa, ooo, and e-vent-u-a-lly you find-you-can-make-words. And if you put the words together that means you can speak and if you do it with other human beings it's called talking to each other and is generally recognised as a very good thing.

Kate *sits silently. She gives him a black look.*

So talk to me.

Kate Fuck off.

Nick (*Michael Caine*) Did you know that the human brain is fifty times superior to that of any other species; that there are nearly two dozen tiny muscles and ligaments in the jaw alone, and all you can come up with is . . .

Kate Nick, please. Give it a rest.

He shrugs and leaves.

Are you all right?

Tish *nods.*

I've said some pretty shitty things. I'm sorry. It's nothing personal. I upset people for a living. As a matter of fact I quite like you, OK?

Tish Thank you.

Kate Do you like me?

Tish No.

Kate Well, fuck you then.

Tish Not much.

She smiles. **Kate** *smiles.*

Kate You're not in a very good state, are you? I'm sorry about your friend.

Tish *sneezes violently, then begins to cry.*

Look, I'm no good with . . . Oh, go on then. It'll do you good. I don't know why, but they say it does.

Tish I'm all right. I just wish . . . I wish we could bury her. They won't let us. They have to keep her, like some sort of evidence or something. I wish we could bury her.

Kate For what it's worth, when my Dad died I kept telling myself I'd feel different after the funeral. He was cremated in Barnes. It's what he wanted. Well, he didn't stipulate Barnes. Anyway, I didn't feel different at all, except that it felt like Sunday all day, but it wasn't. She's gone, so you just have to let her go.

Tish I'm scared.

Kate Well, so am I.

Tish But I'm scared of everybody.

Kate Well, at least now we know what he looks like. Only about seven million men in the country fit the description. He's tall apparently, and gaunt. In his fifties.

Tish I know. I was the one who described him.

Kate Jesus.

Tish This one man would turn up wherever Alison was playing. He was besotted. She got quite fond of him, chatted. I saw them leave together that night. I don't know, he might not have. It could have been anyone. I shouldn't be telling you this. Don't say anything.

Keith *comes on with a variety of ropes and a pair of handcuffs.*

Keith You know you really don't look well. I think you've got what I had last week.

Tish I'm all right. Excuse me.

Keith There's this herbal stuff called EPC. It's great.

Tish *leaves.*

Nick's practising his Woody Allen. I wish I was Woody Allen.

Kate Don't be silly, Keith. What's Woody Allen got that you haven't?

Keith Diane Keaton, Charlotte Rampling, Mia Farrow, Mariel Hemingway. And a Jewish mother. I want a Jewish mother.

Kate Believe me, they're overrated.

Keith Would you help me with this?

He gestures to the ropes and handcuffs. During the scene he will get **Kate** *to tie and handcuff him to a chair.*

I suppose what I really want is to come clean.

Kate How do I do this?

Keith Padlock first, then the ropes.

Kate What do you mean, come clean?

Keith Well, it's a bit rehearsed, I suppose.

Kate What?

Keith Well, it's quite hard to say because I don't know how much you realise. About the way I feel about you.

Pause. **Kate** *pulls a rope around him tightly.*

Had you realised?

Kate Yes, I suppose so. I had really, I suppose.

Keith So I'm coming clean.

Pause She carries on tying.

I might get a bit nervous now.

Kate No, you won't.

Keith I usually do.

Kate Well, don't. (*Pause. She comes close to him in the course of tying.*) God, life's cruel. Thank you for telling me.

Keith I wanted you to know at least. I'm quite together about it, don't worry. If it's a big no just say so. I'm not the sort of frog that gets bigger the longer you refuse to kiss it. I don't want it to get in the way of any friendship we may have, I just think you should know I'd like to sleep with you. I mean I'd love it. And if that feeling's a secret it can mess things up, so it's best that you know, then I know you know, you know?

Kate I'm very flattered.

Keith That's a no if ever I heard one. Don't worry, I didn't expect a yes.

Kate I'm sorry. I wish it could be. If I was someone else and could say, well, we like each other so what the hell, come home tonight, I would. But I'm not. I'm me, and I can't do that. You're very charming. A dreadful magician but very charming and I suppose I like it when you're around but I just don't fancy you.

Keith Aaaargh! That's it. That's what you shouldn't have said. My stomach just imploded.

Kate Look, Keith, I'm sorry. I know how it feels. Believe me I know how it feels in there. But I find it hard to believe I'm the cause of it.

Keith Helen of Troy kept saying that. Handcuffs. Don't worry, I'll survive. I shall pretend we did and it was awful.

Kate Don't do that.

Keith Why not?

Kate Because it fucking well wouldn't be. If we did. But we're not going to.

Keith Gag me will you? Did you know Houdini could get out of any combination of ropes and jacket in thirty seconds?

Kate Well, I wish you the best of luck. (*She has gagged him and now closes the cuffs.*) Go.

She looks at her watch and waits thirty seconds. **Keith** *struggles like mad for fifteen of them, then settles down to a more concentrated effort.*)

Do you mind if I get on with something else?

She sits down with a pad and biro. **Nick** *enters with a cardboard cut-out of Thatcher, which he begins to fix up. Then he puts it aside, sits opposite* **Kate** *and looks at her steadily for some time.*

Nick Well?

Kate What?

Nick Well what? What's wrong?

Kate Nothing.

Nick Oh, come on.

Kate *looks over at* **Keith**.

Talk to me.

Kate Well, aren't you the least bit interested?

Nick In what? What do you mean?

Kate I've been to Brighton.

Nick I know you've been to Brighton. If you spent more time working . . .

Kate Ask me what I've been doing. Ask me what I did in Brighton.

Nick What did you do in Brighton?

Kate I got rid of our child.

Pause.

Nick (*Kirk Douglas*) You mean you had an abortion?

Kate No, I left her at my mother's. Christ.

Nick (*Woody Allen*) Look, er, I always think that, er, there are only two things worth doing before you die, and neither of them is tax deductable.

Kate Nicholas!

Nick Look, I never said I was capable of looking after a kid! I made it perfectly clear it was the wrong time in my life.

Kate Well, me too. So I've taken her to my mother's, God help the kid. But I'm not deserting her. I'll return to Brighton when she's fourteen and help her rebel; I'll be the sort of influence I never had when I was a child. Anyway, so there's no kid around any more. Satisfied?

Nick (*Bogart*) Sure, kid, and this time it'll all be different.

Kate All Pattie would do in Brighton; she wouldn't respond to me, except to hit my knee as hard as she could with her little fists and shout, 'Naughty girl.' All day long, 'Naughty girl.'

Nick Well, she always had immaculate taste in parents.

Kate She'll be happier. I know it. My God, she's got the entire fucking ocean down there.

Nick We'll visit.

Kate You're joking.

Nick Next weekend.

Kate Seriously? Would you?

Nick Kate, I'm not a complete bastard.

Kate Yes, you are. But you do try, I suppose.

Nick (*Basil Fawlty*) Basically I am a trying bastard, yes.

He grabs her suddenly and kisses her. It always works.
Keith's *chair falls over.*

Kate Whoops a daisy. Is that part of it?

Keith (*gagged*) Oh, of course.

Nick Actually you know, this is a better act than your other one.

Nick *puts his arm around* **Kate**. **Keith** *looks away and struggles on.*

Kate Just one thing, though. If we're going to be friends then just be straight with me, OK? Just don't betray me, huh? I've gotten used to most of the shit you put me through but I never get used to that.

Nick (*Tom Conti*) Would I lie to you? (*Himself.*) OK.

Kate You promise?

Nick I promise.

Kate I really wish I didn't.

Nick What?

Kate Nothing.

Enter **Tish**. *Everyone smiles at everyone else.* **Tish** *sits,* **Kate** *returns to her writing, and* **Nick** *proceeds to hang Thatcher from the neck above the stage.*

Tish If you're all busy, perhaps I should go . . .

Kate No, stay. Please. Please.

Pause. **Tish** *settles.*

(*To* **Nick**.) Have you ever heard a woman say cunt?

Nick (*Eric Morecambe*) Pardon?

Kate Cunt. I don't think I've heard a woman say it. Why is that?

Nick (*Noel Coward*) Probably because they never met you.

Kate Ha ha. It's a good word. Cunt. It's strong.

Nick It's awfully rude.

Kate It is since your lot got hold of it. Cunt. Cunt. Fanny, yuk. Whatsit, quim.

Tish I really think I'd better go.

Kate Don't be ridiculous; it's snowing. Orifice! No, we've all got those.

Nick What do you want, words for cunt?

Kate Yes, maybe.

Nick Bush. Hole. Honeypot.

Kate Honeypot? Jesus.

Nick Minge. Mound of Venus.

Kate God, the mind of man.

Nick Doughnut. Love box. Beaver.

Keith (*gagged*) Vagina.

Kate I thought you said it should take about thirty seconds.

Keith (*gagged*) I said it took Houdini thirty seconds.

Nick The Sulphurous Pit. Crotch. Slit.

Tish I'm sorry, I really do have to go. (*She rises.*)

Kate No, please. What's wrong?

Tish I'm sorry, I don't understand why you have to use words like that. They're not particularly funny.

Kate We were thinking aloud. I'm sorry. Please, sit down.

Tish *sits*.

Nick Oyster. Bearded Clam.

Kate Shut up. I've got it anyway.

Tish I suppose you think I'm a bit of a prude, I suppose I am. It's just the way I was brought up.

Kate How were you brought up?

Tish (*smiles*) My mother was a Catholic.

Kate Ahah! All is explained. You were thrown to the nuns.

Tish Twelve years in convent school.

Kate Sounds worse than B'nai Hakiba.

Tish It was awful. For years I had to put my dressing-gown on first and then get undressed for bed; which is actually impossible. What about you?

Kate I survived Leviticus. At sixteen I knew nothing about contraception and all there is to know about leprosy. My idea of rebellion was to be under the covers with a torch reading the New Testament.

Tish I remember in my last year at school I was chosen to play Gabriel. It was the best part. So the night before I curled my hair. The next morning Sister Mary dragged me up to the front of the class and pulled my hair and said I wasn't allowed to play Gabriel; I had to play the ox. She said, 'Angels don't show off!' I thought there's not much point being an angel then, really.

Kate I wish you wouldn't.

Tish What?

Kate You keep making me laugh. I'm supposed to be

the funny one. You're supposed to be the dumb pretty one.

Tish Sorry.

Kate Don't be.

Tish All right.

They smile at each other.

Nick Look, um . . . anyone want to come and play in the snow?

Kate Play in the snow?

Keith (*gagged*) It's no good. I give up. Can someone help me out of this?

Nick Sure. (*Looks at his watch.*) It's half-past six. Come on, Kate. Snowballs.

Kate It's dark; you're crazy.

Nick Come on.

Kate All right. But not down the neck. Tish?

Tish No.

Kate Oh, come on.

Tish I've got a bit of a cold.

Kate Five minutes.

Nick She's got a cold.

Kate All right. It's just you and me, ratface. Hey, what happened?

Nick What?

Kate I'm happy. I'm happy.

Nick *and* **Kate** *leave. After a pause,* **Keith** *tries to smile.*

Keith (*gagged*) Could you help me out of this, please?

Tish *crosses to help* **Keith**.

Tish Oh, I'm sorry. What do I do?

Keith (*inaudible*) Handcuffs!

Tish *tries the cuffs.*

Tish Where's the key?

Keith Well, do the gag first.

Tish Sorry.

She undoes the gag. He sticks out his tongue. On the end of it is the key.

What's it doing in there?

Keith That's where you keep it.

Tish Why?

Keith To do the trick.

Tish How?

Keith I'm not sure. Perhaps you're meant to swallow it and wait a couple of days.

Tish I was never any good with ropes and knots and things. I had a friend, he used to get really frustrated with me.

Keith That's a shame.

Tish Oh no, he liked getting frustrated. (**Tish** *sneezes.*)

Keith Bless you.

Tish Thank you. (*She sneezes again.*)

Keith Would you like a handkerchief?

Tish No, thank you.

Keith Actually this isn't an ordinary handkerchief.

Tish Isn't it?

Keith No, actually it's haunted.

Tish I see.

Keith *does the haunted handkerchief trick.* **Tish** *laughs.*

That's very good.

Keith I'm glad you laughed. I don't think tricks should be taken too seriously, you know what I mean?

Tish Do it again.

Keith No. No. Sorry.

Tish Please. Another one then.

Keith All right, all right. Well, there's one that's a bit silly. It involves us making a bet together. I bet you . . . um . . .

Tish What?

Keith No.

Tish No, go on, what?

Keith Well, I bet you I can kiss you without touching you. I bet you a pound.

Tish Why?

Keith It's a trick. I bet you a pound I can kiss you without touching you.

Tish What do you mean? Where?

Keith On the lips.

Tish You'd touch me on the lips.

Keith No. I'll kiss you on the lips but I won't touch you anywhere.

Tish Not even the lips?

Keith No touching at all.

Tish That's impossible.

Keith It's a trick.

Tish You bet me a pound you can kiss me without touching me? Anywhere?

Keith Yes.

Tish What's the catch?

Keith Well, never mind if you don't want to . . .

Tish No, I'm intrigued. All right, I bet you a pound.

Keith Right. OK. OK. Right. Now you have to sit perfectly still. You mustn't move. Lift your head up and close your eyes.

Tish I'll keep my eyes open if you don't mind.

Keith All right. Ready?

Tish I suppose so.

He kisses her. It's a gentle kiss but shocks her. She pulls away. He hands her a pound.

Keith Worth every penny.

She turns her head away sadly. Aware and concerned that he may have hurt her feelings, he turns her head back to him. He kisses her again. This time she doesn't pull away. **Kate** *returns for her coat.*

Kate Have you two been introduced? Tish, this is Keith, Keith this is Tish. Keith's an old friend of mine who's harboured a deep affection for me for some time. In fact just earlier on he was telling me how much he could do with getting his leg over at the moment. You slimey toe-rag. I almost fell for that shit. At least most men are straightforward bastards, but Christ, the arsenal of lies and smarm some of you bring out when you're desperate . . .

Keith Kate, we were only . . .

Kate I couldn't give a fuck. Go on; if the old friends let you down try for a quick one with some little dip who doesn't know any better. Jesus.

Keith Look, I meant what I said earlier . . .

Kate You didn't mean a fucking word and even if you did, what do I care. I said no. I said no to you, you boring little fart and if you were the last wimp on earth the answer would still be no. No! Never! You are out of the running.

Keith Look, I kissed her because she's pretty. It's easy to fancy her. It's not easy to fancy you, I know that. I'm confused.

Kate How many women have you had, Keith?

Keith Why?

Kate How many?

Keith Seven.

Kate And however many you do have, you will always know the number.

Keith Well, if you're worried about being a statistic I'm surprised you still see so much of him. He keeps a list of the women he's had. It's enormous. And I shouldn't be surprised if he's started a separate column for the names of your close friends. And your not-so-close friends.

Tish *coughs, then sneezes.*

Kate Already? Jesus Christ.

Keith I shouldn't have said anything, I'm sorry.

Keith *leaves.* **Tish** *sneezes again. As the scene continues she gradually declines into quite a bad asthma attack.*

Kate I don't know why I'm surprised. I mean there have been a few. There was a script editor from the BBC called Carol, there was a freelance who interviewed him for *City Limits*, there was Miss Portsmouth nineteen seventy-something; that was quite a big deal. There was some teenager from Webber Douglas and two or three Assembly Room groupies at the Festival this year, and the daughter of a Conservative front-bencher, and my friend Jenny and my other friend Rachel . . . So I really can't understand why I'm so pissed off with you!

Tish I'm sorry.

Kate Except, of course, you've both been lying to me and laughing at me all day!

Tish I haven't . . .

Kate And letting me think that just for once things might be different. Just once I might not be being dumped on.

Nick *appears briefly, unseen by* **Tish** *or* **Kate**. *He hears the row and disappears again.*

Just once I might have met a woman with more interest in me than in him. Just one woman who didn't regard me with complete bloody contempt!

Tish (*with difficulty*) I like you.

Kate Well, I hate your fucking guts. I hate your face and your hair, I hate your sexy little body and your stupid little voice and every last ounce of cuteness in you!

Tish *now has trouble breathing.*

And I hate your bloody hay fever and your coughing and sneezing and the rash on your neck you think you're hiding! And if this is what they call an asthma attack then I have to say that it's pathetically predictable.

Tish *tries to speak but cannot.*

I hope you love him! Because then I can watch him break your fucking heart!

Tish *collapses, sits on the floor.*

Stop it. Stop it! (*She throws a glass of stale beer into* **Tish**'s *face.*)

Tish You're just jealous! I'm pretty. I can't help it, I like it. I'm a pretty girl.

Kate You're a piece of arse. You're meat. It's you that brings the butchers out to play, not me!

A stranger enters. He fits the description we heard earlier.

My, look. A bald, gaunt man, middle fifties. Help yourself. (**Kate** *leaves.*)

The following scene between **Tish** *and the* **Man** *is accompanied by an off-stage argument between* **Kate** *and* **Nick**. *The argument is not completely audible.*

Tish's *body goes rigid when she recognises the* **Man**. *She seems terrified. She has difficulty getting to her feet, but when the* **Man** *takes a step towards her she stumbles backwards, knocks over a chair, and ends up on the floor again.*	**Kate** Nick!
	Nick Ho Ho Ho!
	Kate You sod.
	Nick What?
	Kate I said you sod.
	Nick How charming.
Man Hello, sweetheart.	**Kate** Lying, scheming sod.
Tish Leave me alone!	
The **Man** *crosses to her and kneels down beside her. He helps her sit up so that she can breathe more easily. He looks around and finds her asthma spray. The* **Man** *gives* **Tish** *the spray.* **Tish** *throws it aside. The* **Man** *retrieves it and discovers that it's empty. He finds her bag and looks*	**Nick** Kate . . .
	Kate Don't 'Kate' me!
	Nick Listen . . .
	Kate I've had it with you.
	Nick Calm down.
	Kate Fuck off!
	Nick Just calm down.

in it for another, but finds nothing. He stands and looks for the window in order to open it for some fresh air, but all the windows are boarded up. He helps her stand.)

Tish Leave me alone.

Man Upsadaisy.

Tish I don't want to upsadaisy.

Man You're coming with me.

Tish No!

Man Come on.

Tish But I'm happy here.

Man Come on.

Tish I'm happy here.

Man Shh. Be a good girl. (*The* **Man** *is leading her out.)*

Tish I've got friends here.

Man Shhh. You need some air.

Tish Umm . . .

Man Come on, sweetheart. (*The* **Man** *leads her off.)*

Kate Don't you tell me to calm down!

Nick Well, don't fucking calm down then, I don't care.

Kate I think you're a pig. I think you're a complete pig.

Nick Why?

Kate You know why!

Nick I don't.

Kate You promised me!

Nick Oh fuck.

Kate That's right. Oh fuck.

Nick Kate . . .

Kate Kate's found out. Oh fuck.

Nick Look, who left who?

Kate And I've been back two hours. And you've lied your fucking head off already.

Nick Kate, this is real life, not *Dallas*. Do you think you could keep your voice down?

Kate Don't you tell me what to . . .

Nick Calm down.

Kate No, I won't fucking calm down!

Nick Look . . .

Kate Don't touch me! Don't touch me! And don't bloody walk away from me either!

Nick Sorry.

Kate You don't know the meaning of the word.

Nick I thought we'd made an agreement.

Kate Oh yes, our agreement.

Nick Yes, our agreement.

Kate Your agreement.

Nick Our agreement.

Kate Bollocks to our agreement.

Nick Oh, fine. Kate doesn't like it, bollocks to it. I wish you'd fucking grow up.

Kate What did you say?

Nick I said grow up.

Kate Me grow up?

Nick Yes, you grow up.

Kate You're telling me to grow up.

Nick You're acting like . . .

Kate You're the one who should bloody well grow up! You're the one still chasing girls round the playground!

Nick You're acting like a twelve-year-old.

Kate Come here. Bloody well come here when I'm talking to you!

The argument continues until **Tish** *and the* **Man** *have gone. Then* **Nick** *evidently walks away from* **Kate** *and back into the room where he savagely lays into the cardboard cut-out.* **Kate** *follows him in.*

Kate If you want me to act like an adult, then start acting like one yourself!

Nick Actually, calling you a child is unfair to children. I'd say your problem is you're stuck in adolescence. Just don't bloody tell me to grow up, all right!

Kate *has noticed* **Tish**'s *absence.*

Kate Where's Tish?

Nick Grow up yourself.

Kate Where's Tish? Nick, where is she?

Kate *checks the back room.* **Keith** *enters from the main doors with a microphone which he puts into the stand.* **Kate** *returns and rushes out of the main doors. We hear her run down a few stairs.*

(*Off.*) Tish! (**Kate** *returns.*) Have you seen Tish? Keith, have you seen her?

Keith Er, yeah. She was downstairs with some bloke.

Kate *turns again.*

You won't catch her. They were driving off in a BMW.
Tasty motor.

Kate *sits quietly, very worried.*

Nick It'll probably be a full house tonight. We've had
a block booking from EXIT. I hope you decide to be
funny.

*Lights fade. Sound of audience chattering. Lights up. It is
a few hours later and* **Kate** *stands in a spotlight in the
middle of her routine. She is initially drunk and punchy,
full of a nervous sort of confidence, making much of it up.*

Kate . . . who the fuck wants to be Felicity Kendal
anyway? I mean, nowadays if a bloke ejaculates
prematurely you have to respect him for it! Coming
before your zip's undone is the sensitive thing to do,
right?

Male Heckler Balls.

Kate New balls. Match point. You know, it used to
worry me that there was no female equivalent for balls.
I was thinking about it earlier. A bloke has got a lot of
balls, right? So what does a good woman have a lot of?
She can't have a lot of tit, because that's male territory;
they stole that word already. Have you noticed how
they hate us to use that word? You only have to
mention your tits and it's:

'Don't say that.'
'What?'
'Don't call them that.'
'Don't call what what?'
'Your tits, don't call your tits er, that.'

'Darling, you are really getting on my mammary glands.
We'll strike a deal. I'll call this a breast and you a tit,
how's that?'

Anyway, they also stole the word cunt. A man's got
balls and that's good, but it's tricky for a woman to

have cunt. She can be one, as most men will tell you, but she can't have one. She has to have a vagina. It used to worry me but I finally worked it out. What women have got a lot of, if men have got a lot of balls, what we've got a lot of is, we've got a lot of clit. Clit. Anyone find clit unacceptable? You need a lot of clit to stand up and say clit in a place like this, you know? Could that be because no man ever said it? Well, one thing's for sure, there are men who are the biggest breasts you could meet, and there are some who are right vaginas, but no man ever had an ounce of clit in him. Clit power!

All right, I want hands up all the women here tonight who, in the middle of a conversation about Kierkegaard or Mahatma Gandhi or bloody Buñuel, have come on? I don't know about you but I only ever come on in white shorts, tube trains, and the flats of total strangers. And it's never the right-on strangers who keep the Tampax on the back of the loo; it's the ones who have spotless bathrooms with cheese-plants. While you're looking for the Tampax you find out how they keep it so spotless. You open the bathroom cabinet and Boots' warehouse falls into the bath. But the worst time . . . have you ever tried finding a box of Tampax at eight-thirty on a Saturday night in an Indian supermarket? You never know if they'll be under the Domestos or next to the Alpen. At least in Sainsbury's they're always in the same place. Hidden behind the sugar. Oh, the curse. (*She takes a drink.*) Have you ever had a bloke undress you and he's got this fantastic tongue? It's been down your throat and in your ear and you've gotten over the initial nausea and think you could be on to a good thing . . . But you feel you ought to tell him so you say, 'I think I ought to tell you; I've got my period.' Then you ask a really silly question. You say, 'Do you mind?' It's a stupid question because the answer is always the same: 'Of course I don't mind. Of course I don't. Christ, is it one o'clock already? Look, I have to sign on in the morning . . .' Blood without violence; nice, warm harmless bleeding. Freaks 'em.

In fact a lot of things to do with sex freak men out, have you noticed? However hip they may be. You know the type who think contraception is sexy? 'Hey baby, you want to put my rubber on?' Sure, you want to put my cap in? No way. Get thee to a lavatory. Men are definitely squeamish about any aspect of sex that doesn't go bumpity bumpity. At bumpity bumpity they're great for short and concentrated periods of time, but most exploration is definitely out. Personally, I measure a man's sensitivity and his degree of sensual and spiritual enlightenment by how much he'll let you fool around with his arsehole. 'Hey, what are you doing? Fuck off!'

It just doesn't work both ways, men do not like to be played around with. They do not like their willies waggled. Show me a flaccid willy and I have this uncontrollable urge to waggle it. 'What the fuck are you doing?' 'I don't know, I just wondered how far it would . . .' (*She mimes stretching it and letting it go like a pinball handle.*)

I don't know, that's their problem. My problem, and here we get to the nitty gritty as far as I can see it, my problem is however right on I get, however much feminism I absorb and believe in and act on, and I do, I am a feminist, but I'm also a heterosexual; so however strong I get there's still a part of me that just wants to be fucked. It just wants to lie there and get screwed around with. I mean even if you take the initiative, somehow you still end up being the fuckee and not the fucker.

A **Heckler** *blows a raspberry.*

Can you make that noise with your mouth as well?

Heckler Sexist crap.

Kate Oh good, I love an intellectual audience. Are you on your own or is that your girlfriend trying to hide under the table?

Heckler You are actually a liability to the Women's Movement.

Kate What does she do, fuck you for practice?

Heckler Inverted pornography!

Kate Oh shut up. Just fucking shut up . . . umm . . . (*She loses her place and some of her poise. A strange pause.*) I know. I know. Has any man ever dragged you to one of those dreadful killer thrillers? You know, Saturday the Fourteenth Part Thirteen, free pair of 3D glasses and a meat skewer on your way in. The left-hand side of the auditorium has been reserved for those members of the audience who would prefer not to go up in smoke. It's always the same: some seven-foot retard stabbing and shooting and drilling his way through the Class of '83, Normal Town High, Mid-America. Where the guys spend all their time talking about the girls and the girls spend all their time taking showers. It's the Black and Decker school of suspense. And these dumb women and their dumb kid sisters have pyjama parties and watch Frankenstein on TV while one by one they're decapitated in Daddy's convertible or roasted in the microwave. And the thing is it has to be a surprise who's doing it. It's got to be the little bloke with glasses or his mother, or it's got to be the heroine's boyfriend . . . someone this last surviving, blood-spattered, half-naked woman is going to run to for help in the final minutes and almost get her throat cut and she'll have to resort to a slow-motion knitting needle through the brain or chop his head off. That last bit's the only bit I enjoy. I have this fantasy, I want to make one. I want to make a killer thriller where they've got the bloke who's been doing it, they've snapped his drill off, there's blood all over the place and they slowly pull off his rubber mask . . . and find a complete and utter stranger.

A no one. Never seen him before. End of film.
Wouldn't that make a crappy thriller? (*Pause.*) But
that's how it happens. It's always some stranger . . .
(*Pause.*) Some bloke . . . (*Pause.*) Ummm . . . Sorry.
(*She loses it.*)

Heckler Boring!

Kate Boring. Right. Umm . . .

Pause. She is not with it now. If **Nick** *or* **Keith** *is visible
they show slight concern.*

That's right, there's only one sin, isn't there? Thou
shalt not be boring. You can be racist, sexist, downright
bad, but if you're boring it's not show business. I'll tell
you why you're bored. You're bored because I'm a
woman, you can't see my tits, and nobody's about to
dismember me. I only talk about it, right? Jesus, he's
right. I give it to you verbally. That's what he meant,
right? All right, I admit it. Guilty. I'm guilty. OK. So,
no more rude words. I promise. No more porn. So,
what now? (*Pause.*)

Heckler Boring!

Kate So now I'm boring! Whoops. Oh fuck, I'm
boring. And guilty. And you paid to get in. That's the
next point you're going to bring up, right? Your petty
fucking admission. All right, what do you want? What
do you want? You want the strip? Tits and arse? Hard
fucking cheese. Right, this is what you get in the
movies. (*She disappears and reappears with a large
cleaver.*) OK. No more boredom. Promise. I'll do the
butcher routine for you. There was a German artist
resorted to this. Listen. Listen to me! People didn't like
this German artist's performance pieces. They didn't
'get' them. So he thought up something more direct;
something they'd be sure to get. He began to cut off his
toes. Then when no one got that he began to cut off his
fingers. That was his gig. He'd do some stuff, then cut
off another finger. And still no one knew what the fuck

he was on about. So finally in a small cellar club in
Berlin in 1951 he surgically removed his own arm. Sold
out that gig. And everyone had stopped giving a shit
what it meant anyway. Off came the arm. Then he died,
which was a shame because he'd been offered a season.
Just him and an industrial mincer. But it's true, the rest
of it. That's what the people wanted. They were bored.
He did his best.

So . . . what I want is a show of hands . . . I need a
good majority, but if I get it I'll give you a finger. Or if
it's unanimous a whole hand. No, perhaps not a whole
hand. But a finger. Hands up for a finger. My finger,
promise. (*Pause.*) No takers. Houseful of humanitarians
is what we have here. Or could it be a houseful of sick,
voyeuristic trendies who are too shy to put up their
pandies? OK, let's turn it around. I want a majority of
hands in the air or you get a finger whether you like it
or not. (*Pause.*) Come on. A couple of hands. Anyone?
(*Pause.*) OK. In all seriousness. Deadly seriousness. I've
got a finger at stake here. If the majority of you will not
put your hands in the air I shall cut my pinky off. I
never use it anyway. It has no function. Come on, I
want hands. I'm serious. I mean it. No joke. Hands up
unless you want me to maim myself for you. You've got
thirty seconds.

Pause. A long one. **Kate** *picks up the cleaver and waggles
her little finger.* **Harry**'*s hand goes up.* **Nicks**'*s hand goes
up.* **Keith**'*s hand is already up.*

Thank you. That's nice of you. Four, no five hands out
of what? A hundred and fifty? Thank you. Five kind
hands. Not enough. (*She brings the cleaver down on her
finger. There is general consternation.*) Is anyone still
bored?

Nick *jumps onstage but she swings the cleaver lazily to
keep him away.*

Careful. I'm probably famous now. All I need is a

pianist. And er . . . wow. Pain is always such a fucking surprise, isn't it? Every time. Well, I reckon I've got a good nine gigs left and then there's a problem. Tuesday week I shall have run out of bookings and won't be able to sign my dole card. Ow! Jesus.

She collapses. **Nick** *runs to her and is generally useless.* **Harry** *is the one who picks her up.*

Harry (*to* **Nick**) Get rid of them.

Nick *looks blankly at* **Harry**.

Clear the bloody room.

Keith Does it hurt?

Kate Only when I laugh.

Kate *passes out.* **Harry** *picks her up . . . The lights fade.*

When the lights come up again ten minutes have passed. The room is empty but for **Kate**, **Harry** *and* **Keith**. **Harry** *has almost completed bandaging* **Kate**'s *hand.* **Keith** *is showing her a trick. He completes it.*

Kate Do it again.

Does it.

Do it again.

Does it.

Do it again.

Does it.

Ow!

Harry Sorry.

Kate How's it done?

Keith Ahah.

Kate Fuckwit.

Keith I don't know why it irritates people so much

that I won't tell them. I've had whole relationships go west because I wouldn't tell them how some stupid trick's done.

Kate Because it's bloody infuriating.

Keith But if I do tell, they're so unimpressed they tend to lose interest anyway. (**Keith** *sits in the corner.*)

Harry How's that?

Kate Thank you.

Nick *enters, white as a sheet.*

Nick They're on their way. It's fucking bedlam down there.

Harry OK. Sit with her. (*Exit* **Harry.**)

Nick I don't know what to say really. I'm irresponsible. I lied to you. I lie to you. A lot. I don't take you seriously. Or Pattie. And I fuck around. I admit it. I fuck around. But you shouldn't have done that.

Kate What?

Nick The thing is . . . I really like making love to women. Different women. I mean there are so many of you. I mean, remember the first time? It's always best that first time. Isn't it?

Kate No.

Nick Well, for us, for me. Look, what I'm trying to say. . . Whatever I do, whatever I am . . . you and I . . . you didn't have to do that.

Kate This may come as a hell of a shock, but I didn't do it because of you.

Nick Mmmm? Sure.

Kate As a matter of fact, I meant to miss.

Nick *looks at her in disbelief, then laughs.*

Ha ha.

He kisses her.

And who was that?

Nick No one.

Kate That doesn't mean it was you, Nick, that means it was no one. No, don't touch me. I don't think I want you to touch me ever again, thank you. In fact, if you so much as lay a finger on me . . . (*She smiles.*) I'll remove it.

They stare at each other. Enter **Harry.**

Harry There's a vanload of black fellers just arrived. They want to talk to you.

Nick Shit.

Harry And it's gone last orders.

Exit **Nick.** **Harry** *looks out of the window.*

Kate Keith?

Keith Yeah?

Kate Show me that trick again.

He does.

And again.

He does.

And again.

He does.

Yeah, I saw it that time.

Harry I think he's going to have some trouble with that big one. I think he could do with some moral support.

Keith Right. Um. Right. (*Exit* **Keith.**)

Kate Thank you, Harry.

Harry I think you should take some advice. I think
you should take a good look at yourself and tell yourself
quite honestly what it is you don't like about yourself.
And you know what it'll be? If you're truly honest
you'll find the thing you don't like about yourself is
your dreadful haircut. Take my advice and grow your
hair. Long. Like it was when you were a girl. You'll feel
a new woman.

An ambulance is heard in the distance. **Kate** *smiles tightly
and makes a rude gesture.*

Harry Two minutes princess, then you'll be on your
way.

Harry *leaves.* **Kate** *surveys the damage to her hand,
takes a drink of the brandy beside her. The* **Man** *enters.
She freezes.*

Man Are you Kate?

Kate Where's Tish?

Man She asked me to come. We left some of her
things.

Kate Who are you?

Man I'm her father. Are you all right?

Kate Where is she?

Man The Kensington. She's had a rather bad attack.
You must have realised how ill she is; it astonishes me
none of you did anything for her.

Kate Well, what's wrong with her?

Man One doctor put it quite succinctly. He said for
some girls there comes a time when the body turns
against the mind and says, 'Enough. I want to stop this
now.' Evidently it's becoming quite common in one
form or another. Patricia said you were a friend of hers.

She asked me to give you this. (*He hands* **Kate** *a note.*)
I've been looking for her since the end of summer. I'm
taking her home, or at least somewhere she can breathe.
Thank you for taking such good care of her.

He takes **Tish**'s *things and leaves.* **Kate** *reads the note.*
Harry *returns.*

Harry Any minute now.

Kate You know the trouble with me, Harry? I get so
angry I don't know who I hate.

Harry It's snowing again. Roads'll be bad.

The lights fade.

Epilogue

A cottage on Dartmoor. The furnishings are very sparse and are all made of wood, stone, or natural wool and cottons. The wind can be heard. **Kate** *is there, dressed against the weather. She has just arrived.*

Tish (*off*) What are you wearing?

Kate What? Oh, um . . . (*She takes off her parka.*) I don't know.

Tish (*off*) It's only wool or cotton, I'm afraid. Anything nylon or acrylic or anything . . .

Kate Shit.

Tish (*off*) I'm sorry.

Kate No, it's all right. I didn't think. (*Looking at the labels of her clothes,* **Kate** *finds she has to strip down to her underwear. This she does with increasing reluctance. The cottage is very cold.*)

Tish (*off*) I'm really sorry. There's a bin liner on the chair.

Kate Don't apologise. Look, the rest's Marks and Spark's. One hundred per cent cotton. Promise.

Tish *comes in, dressed simply in white and looking very well.*

Tish I'm sorry. Here. (*She offers her a sheet.*)

Kate Hello.

Tish Hello.

Kate You're looking well.

Tish I am well. That's why I'm being so careful.

Daddy's spent a fortune on this place. He comes up all he can. And there's a girl in the village who rides up every other day . . .

Kate You must be lonely as hell.

Tish But I'm well. Breathe. Just breathe. Isn't the air wonderful?

Kate Not all over.

Tish Are you cold? I've gotten used to the cold.

Kate Well, it's all right for you. You've got more clothes on than usual. I'm sorry about that awful day. Nick's gone to New York to be famous now. Keith's doing TIE in Watford. The circuit took over the pub; now it's all slagging off the Left or putting fish down your trousers really.

Tish How's your hand?

Kate Oh, healing. It'll be OK. God, it's quiet. What do you do out here on your own?

Tish I look out of the window. The night I arrived I couldn't sleep so I got up and tried to see out; but it was very black. Cold. All I could see was my own reflection in the glass. So I sat there and looked at myself until morning. And as the sun came up I began to fade away and beyond the glass the most fantastic landscape happened. The view is wonderful. I used to spend a lot of time looking in mirrors; preparing myself, beautifying. Then I'd do the act and they'd all agree I was very special and I'd smile and go back to the mirror. Now I spend all that time at the window, or the one in the other room. Sometimes as it gets dark I begin to see myself again . . . but there's no need to look any more. I turn on the lights and read a book. Would you like some tea?

Kate Thanks.

Tish *goes to the door.*

Tish?

Tish Yes?

Kate Umm . . .

Kate *fights back tears. With great relief,* **Tish** *runs to comfort her. They kiss each other.*

Tish Think of a colour.

Kate What?

Tish Close your eyes and think of a colour. (**Tish** *presses her forehead tightly to* **Kate**'s *for five or six seconds then pulls away.*) Yellow.

Kate That's astonishing. Do it again.

They repeat the procedure.

Tish Pink.

Kate I don't believe it.

Tish It's easy. It's obvious really; that's where you think, so if you put them together and think hard enough . . . You try it. Just make your mind blank for a second, then try it.

Kate (*tries it, then with great hesitation*) Blue. Blue?

Tish *smiles.*

Tish Blue.

Kate Sky blue or sea blue?

Tish Sky blue. (*Pause.*) You will stay for a while, won't you?

Kate I have to go to Brighton. Come with me.

Slow fade.

Cries from the Mammal House

For Ken Campbell and Neil Oram

'God help thee, old man, thy thoughts have created a creature in thee.'

Herman Melville, *Moby Dick*

Cries from the Mammal House was first presented by Open Hearted Enterprises in a co-production with the Royal Court Theatre and the Haymarket Theatre, Leicester, at the Haymarket Theatre, Leicester, on 5 April 1984, with the following cast:

David	Roger Rees
Alan	David Lyon
Anne	Jennie Stoller
Sally	Lorraine Brunning
Mick	Tim Roth
Nirad	Nizwar Karanj
Lei	Sarah Lam
Victor	Leo Wringer
Palmer	David Lyon
Mrs Palmer	Jennie Stoller

Directed by Phil Young
Designed by Peter Hartwell
Costumes by Andrew Dickson

The first performance of this production at the Royal Court Theatre, London, was on 3 May 1984.

Characters

David   *Mid thirties. English born but Welsh bred which has left him with an accent. He is fated with uncontrollable hair which, however old he gets, will always mean he looks like a Lost Boy.*

Alan   *David's brother. No accent. Late thirties. A gaunt, tense man.*

Anne   *Mid thirties. Married to Alan. Intense, tall, dark.*

Sally   *Sixteen. Daughter to Alan and Anne. Small for her age and not too pretty, not too plain.*

Mick   *Seventeen. The build, but not the face, of a bully.*

Nirad   *A young, thin Hindu. Nineteen or so. Looks quite incredibly innocent.*

Lei   *Nineteen. A Chinese woman. A face that never smiles.*

Victor *A creole, similar in build to Mick.*

Palmer *Late forties, distinguished-looking. Played by the actor who plays Alan.*

Mrs Palmer   *Sad-looking woman in her forties. Dresses out-of-date. Played by the actress who plays Anne.*

Setting

The first and last parts of the play are set in a small provincial zoo in England. The middle part is set in a large colonial house and various other locations on the island of Mauritius. Locations therefore have to be minimal, the stage space flexible, but the following features are absolutely necessary:

Enormous flat surfaces of concrete and pastel-painted steel as used in zoos of the fifties: reference the paintings, of Gilles Aillaud
Stuffed and mounted animals and birds: as many as possible

The quality of the action in the first and last sections is sparse and coldly lit. The middle section by comparison has a dreamlike quality, not to indicate an idyll, but to suggest the less rational areas of the mind are at work.

Note: all live animals should be invisible, and mimed by the actors. All dead animals, in whatever condition, should be present.

Act One

England

Scene One

The mammal house

Anne, *alone, stares straight ahead of her, directly to the audience.*

Anne Listen! This isn't the real world. This is a zoo. You think you'd prefer the real world? Foraging for yourself instead of opening that mouth for whatever we choose to drop into it? Nothing but nature between you and the horizon? You dream of it as a sort of freedom, the real world? Elephants might fly. Let me tell you, when we stole it from you, this dream of yours, the weapon we used was our intelligence. And now the world's been stolen from us by a small élite of our own species and the weapon they used was money. So we sit in our enclosures, our horizons painted on glass, our mouths wide open . . . but instead of education, self-respect and common decency, we are fed television, charge cards and bloody families. Oh, and not forgetting love of course. We're fed a lie called love. It's something you fall in. Anyway, I hope you're grateful at least for civilisation. You'd be behind bars without it. We've done away with the bars and the netting. Nothing obscures the view. You only know you're in a cage if you try to leave it.

Enter **Alan** *in a white coat.*

He joins his wife and they gaze in the same direction.

Alan There's nothing I can do.

Anne You could do nothing, but that would be far too assertive for you. You'll do what you're told and shoot her, won't you?

Alan If I don't, somebody else will.

Anne That was never any excuse and never bloody will be.

Alan I'm a qualified surgeon. I can kill her more humanely than any policeman.

Anne I'm a qualified psychotherapist. I could do a better lobotomy than a butcher. But I won't.

He takes off his white coat and offers her a black armband. She ignores it.

How long does it take a body to rot?

Alan What, my father?

Anne How long, until he's rotten?

Alan (*taking a breath*) About two years I suppose.

Anne Perhaps then I'll mourn. (*She leaves.*)

Alan *faces front.*

Alan What do you want? I've nothing to give you. Listen, I don't talk to animals, but what I'm trying to say is, we don't forget either, all right? So I'm sorry. (*He reaches out his hand.*)

David (*off*) Is anybody there?

There is an echo. The elephant trumpets. Another echo.

Alan *pulls his hand away a little gingerly.*

Enter **David** *with an overnight bag.*

Alan I'm here.

David Weddings and funerals eh? I got a taxi from the station.

Alan Hello.

David Hello.

They shake hands. **David** *embraces* **Alan.**

I'll be late for my own as well.

Alan How are you?

David Bloody fantastic, how are you?

Alan Bloody miserable.

David Oh, he had a good run for his money.
Considering none of it was his, a bloody good run. He
was a fine man.

Alan Was he?

David I don't know, was he?

Alan No.

David That's what I thought. Being the bastard son I
always put it down to resentment, this feeling that he
was . . . an ignorant son of a bitch.

Alan No, he was an ignorant son of a bitch.

David Yes?

Alan Yeh.

David Greedy, avaricious . . .

Alan You said it.

David Bastard.

Alan Right.

David Still, mustn't speak ill of the dead.

Alan I never loved him, but he was always there. Old
sod was always there and now he's gone. I had a father
and now I don't and there's no flesh between me and
the grave.

David I know what you mean. My mother died. Heart attack on the tractors. I've got a farm now.

Alan I've got a zoo.

David Is that her?

Alan *nods.*

A pause as they look at her. She moves in the shadows.

Bloody silly way to go, wasn't it?

They both laugh.

What really happened?

Alan Just what you heard. It was Sally's birthday. She's sixteen now. We've been hiring out the reptile house or the aquarium recently: you know, law firms' Christmas parties, trendy christenings. So the old man decided we'd have Sally's birthday bash in the mammal house. And he got drunk and arrogant as usual; ranted on about his pissy little zoo as if it were still the best in Britain and dragged Sally around with him like some new acquisition.

David The elephant was the first wasn't it?

Alan Yes. Ellie put us on the map by all accounts. Back in '49. They walked her up from the docks as a publicity stunt. There's a photo that hangs in the office . . .

David I've seen it.

Alan Her and the old man. He was what, forty?

David In a suit and tie, holding out a contract for the elephant to sign. Bloody silly.

Alan Anyway, he got it into his head to take another photograph at the party. Twenty-five years – a wonderful partnership, silly sod. He hadn't been in an enclosure for fifteen of them, least of all hers. He wouldn't know if an animal wanted to fondle him or tear his bloody head off, but he wouldn't be stopped; he

clambered in with her. She was calm. Wouldn't give
him her trunk though, she just stood there thinking.
Then she turned, lifted him clean off the floor and
threw him into the moat. Broke his spine. As you said.
Bloody silly.

David What now then?

Alan I have to shoot her.

David Oh come on man, it must have been an
accident. A pretty spectacular one, I admit . . .

Alan She did it on purpose.

David Elephants don't kill. Why would she?

Alan (*suddenly angry*) How the hell should I know?

David You're supposed to be an animal lover.

Alan No, you're supposed to be an animal lover. I'm a
surgeon. I was trained at great expense to keep these
furry little, big leather toys eating and shitting well into
their natural span. And sometimes I go and masturbate
a panda or inseminate a baboon; anything to keep this
bloody place alive. I'm no longer an animal lover.

David Liar.

Enter **Anne.**

Anne Are you two going to carry this bloody coffin?

David I suppose we'd better. If we leave it much
longer he'll probably get up and walk.

Anne Hello.

David Hello.

Anne Where have you been?

David I came as soon as I heard. I was on a field trip.
I'd built myself such a good hide no one could tell
where I was. Except all the bloody birds of course.

Alan Let's get this done shall we? (**Alan** *moves off.*)

David How are you?

Anne Oh, life goes on doesn't it?

David I suppose it does really, touch wood.

He touches her head. She responds as if it were a light electric shock.

Where's Sally?

Anne Who's Sally?

David Is she coming?

Anne She'll make up her own mind. She usually does.

David Where is she?

Anne In a world of her own, David. In a world of her own. (*She goes.*)

David *turns to the elephant's enclosure.*

David This could be very depressing.

Scene Two

Somewhere in the zoo. Late night.

Sally *enters as a kangaroo, followed by* **Mick**. *He has an Adidas bag with football boots attached.*

Sally Take off your clothes.

Mick What?

Sally Go on.

Mick Why?

Sally All of them.

Mick No.

Sally Go on.

Mick Why?

Sally You know. You first.

He takes off most of his clothes.

Mick This is fucking stupid. All right, your turn.

She doesn't respond.

He tries to kiss her but she runs away. He tries again, but again she escapes him. He begins to dress.

She takes off her knickers.

He undresses again to his underpants and socks. He takes a step towards her but she shakes her head.

She circles him. Her movements become more and more ape-like until she is quite accurately impersonating a chimpanzee.

He is confused and embarrassed as she circles him. He will not join in the game.

She offers him her backside, he walks towards her normally, she runs away from him.

Finally his desire wins over his embarrassment and he joins in. They both become apes in a ritual courtship. They end up in the mating position. **Mick** *begins to undress* **Sally** *from behind. When they are both very excited, he turns her around to kiss her. She pushes him away violently and, becoming human again, walks away.*

Sally Chimpanzees don't do it like that.

Mick Well, I'm not a fucking chimpanzee. (*He gets dressed.*)

Sally Did you know there was a swift they found and its little ring told them that the little swift had flown to the moon and back. Eight times. All in one little lifetime; enough miles to visit the moon. And there's a toad, the Gobi toad, who takes one look at the Gobi and buries himself in it until the rains come. Seven years it takes the rain to come, seven years the Gobi toad stays buried in the sand. Then the rains fall and the toad comes up and makes love in the rain. And the swift makes love on the wing. And snails slip from their shells to spiral one another and hang and dance on threads of juice as one loves the other and the other loves the first. And penguins get married for life; they never fall out because they only see each other for three months every year. The rest of the time they swim in the ice cold sea and do jokes for one another. And did you know that a horse's thing, when it's up, is bigger than a whale's? And a tomcat's thing has sharp hairs on it pointing up to keep it in, and that's why she-cats scream.

Mick Who told you all this stuff?

Sally Grandpa.

Mick Dirty old sod.

Sally He's dead now.

Something falls out of **Mick**'s *pocket.*

What's this?

Mick Nothing.

Sally Your report.

Mick Give it here.

Sally English Lit. No concentration, no application and quite frankly no ability. D.

Mick Yeh, D, D, D, C minus, what the fuck.

Sally Mathematics. 'Michael who?'

Mick Fucking cheek.

Sally F. Biology. A glimmer of application when dissecting, but otherwise sadly inept. C minus.

Mick PE. B!

Sally B minus. Lateness and lack of discipline mar

Michael's obvious talents in this field.

Mick Cheeky bastard.

Sally Art: A plus.

Mick What? (*He snatches the report.*)

Sally Anyone can do art.

Mick Oh yeah?

Sally General comment: no comment.

Mick Bunch of comedians.

Sally What'll you do?

Mick I'll get a job.

Sally There are no jobs.

Mick I'll get one.

Sally What sort of job is there for a quite good footballer who likes cutting up frogs?

Mick Look, I'll get a job, OK? I'm up for a few as it happens. (*He takes out some Job Centre cards.*) Allied Carpets, Dewhurst's, Burton's – no, fuck that – Sainsbury's, Sainsbury's and Sainsbury's. Give us a kiss.

Sally No.

Mick Kiss me.

Sally No.

Mick Why not?

Sally I don't like it. I don't like that sort of thing.

Mick Well, what we were doing just then?

Sally Animals. I like animals.

Scene Three

An indoor enclosure that is now a storeroom. Shelf after shelf of stuffed and mounted animals.

Anne *in the middle, disorientated, unsure of where to begin.* **David** *on the outskirts, watching.*

She picks up a small bird with some distaste and throws it into a tea-chest. She throws a small alligator after it, and a stoat.

David I'll have ten quid on the alligator. This is a bloody mausoleum, isn't it?

Anne I'm sorry about dinner.

David That's all right. I only became a vegetarian because some smart Alec handed me a live chicken and said, 'I'll peel the potatoes, you do that.'

Anne I meant the row.

David I refuse to get involved.

Anne The place won't run itself. (*She throws away an owl.*)

David It must feel a bit unnatural like, stepping straight into his father's shoes. He's just being a bit respectful, that's all.

Anne He's being a wimp. He's not in mourning for your father, he's in mourning for his own life. He worked for that man for twenty years and never had a thought of his own. I've watched this place deteriorate from a healthy zoo with the best breeding record in Europe to a prison so penniless a third of the cages are empty. The toucan is actually mouldy. Not because Alan's a bad vet, although he is, he is a bad vet, but because the heating's so ancient the humidity's all to pot. There's a dead toad in the reptile house the size of a kitten. It's been there for a week. No one's noticed it and I'm not telling them. There's so much decay here David, you wouldn't believe it.

David It's not Alan's fault. It's money, isn't it?

Anne If he'd taken over when I told him to, his father wouldn't have had the chance to wreck the place. That man would throw a banquet every month and redecorate his home every year, sod the birds strangling themselves in a decrepit aviary, sod making the lion house safe.

David Isn't it?

Anne It's not even safe for the lions. This used to be a happy place. The designs were revolutionary, and the moats, the freedom. It was a good zoo.

David There's no such thing.

Anne It was a good zoo!

David I prefer my animals hard to find. Anyway, I don't envy you. I wouldn't run a place like this if you asked me.

Anne What if I did? Ask you?

David I wouldn't.

Anne There's good work you could be doing here. We've got a pair of condors.

David Not in the same cage you haven't. They'd tear each other's heads off. No, captivity work depresses me. If it was up to me I'd do a St Francis of Assisi and open every cage.

Anne Then what?

David I'd get the fuck out of there. The great thing about animals is they have no table manners. A wild animal looks at you and you look back and in its eyes there's either fear or hunger, nothing else. You're in a forest with a miracle that's pure fright, flight, and appetite, and it knows the forest better than you ever will.

She offers him a stuffed animal.

No thanks.

Anne Put it in the box.

David Look, I'm sorry but I won't touch anything that's had that done to it.

Anne Anything died, he'd have it stuffed. And the meat roasted for his gourmets' circle.

David You're joking.

Anne I'm serious. Every little death carefully tasted by the wealthy people and then preserved for God knows what reason. Property I suppose; if it's not rotten you can still own it. I'm going to burn the bloody lot.

Enter **Alan**.

Alan Oh.

Anne What?

Alan Do you think you should?

Anne Do you think I should what?

Alan Um . . .

Anne Go away.

Alan *goes*.

Anyway, how are you? (*She throws away a bird*.)

David So so.

Anne Busy?

David I've run out of birds. It's the Armageddon panic. There's not a breeding pair of any endangered species without twenty pairs of Boots binoculars trained on them.

Look, I've been dying to tell you: if I've seemed a bit more buoyant than I should have it's because I finally got the project grant. I'm off to Mauritius. There are more endangered species of bird there than anywhere. . Have you ever seen a Mauritius kestrel?

Anne No.

David Then you won't. It's gone. Finished. And four years ago they were still in the air, a few of them, flying. There are these Pink Pigeons see: I think I can save them, but it's been a hell of a job getting any money because there's so few no one thinks it's possible. But if they're on the wing, then it bloody well is possible. Anything's possible.

Anne A place where anything's possible?

David It's a special place. There was a plant discovered there only twenty years ago: it blooms in November; it's got a beautiful orange flower; I can't describe it. But it's a female and as far as anyone knows, there's only one, no male. So it'll bloom a few more times and that'll be it. I want to see that flower. I'll send you a polaroid if you like.

Anne *turns away from him.*

David I knew it; you're a closet human being after all. (*He touches her, tender, sexual.*)

Anne Don't! Just . . . get the hell out of here. Don't waste your time; I don't want to feel anything. Everything hurts and I wish I were dead, so just leave me alone. Go on. Fuck off and save the world.

David *goes.* **Anne** *uncovers one of the few exhibits protected from the dust. She finds a dodo.*

Scene Four

Somewhere in the zoo. Late evening.

Enter **Sally** *wearing 3D glasses and pretending to be a lizard.*

Mick *suddenly leaps out from behind something, brandishing a large meat knife and yelling some obscenity from a shock-horror film.* **Sally** *takes little notice.*

Sally I hate that sort of film.

Mick It was great. A great film that.

Sally He killed that little dog.

Mick He strangled her father with a cheese wire, he cut off her mother's arms and you're upset that he killed the fucking dog!

Sally Well that's different. Dogs don't get on your nerves like parents.

Mick Fucking great film.

Sally Where'd you get that?

Mick That's the surprise.

Sally It's a horrible surprise.

Mick A bloke wants a job, he's got to have tools.

Sally You stole those; you stole them from the animal kitchen.

Mick The bloke takes a thing, he chops it up, he feeds it to another thing. The bloke's in full employment.

Sally You put them back or I'll tell.

Mick You do and I'll chop your fucking head off. Look, keep it quiet. I stand a better chance with my own tools. (*He adds a couple of knives and a smaller cleaver to the collection.*)

He tries to kiss her. She avoids him. They sit for a while.

Sally Mick.

Mick What? . . . What?

Sally Praying mantis.

Mick Praying what?

Sally Mantis.

Mick Fucking hell.

Sally Please.

Mick Not insects now?

Sally The male creeps up on the female while she's praying. From behind.

Mick So what's new? Couldn't we just . . .

Sally No. I told you I hate all that boy-girl stuff.

She prays, bending over and moving her bum up and down slowly. **Mick** *walks up and fondles her bum.*

Sally Will you stop fooling around!

Mick What'd I do?

Sally A praying mantis does not fondle its mate's bum. Its mate hasn't got a bum to fondle and it has nothing to fondle with and anyway you didn't approach me properly.

Mick I feel a right tit doing this.

Sally Like a mantis.

Mick OK. Like a friggin' mantis.

She prays. He preys. Once again, he joins her from behind and they copulate. She turns part way around and takes up the large carving knife. **Mick** *suddenly finds it held to his neck.*

Mick Sally!

Sally Don't stop.

Mick Fucking hell.

Sally Keep going. It's a habit of the female mantis. As he makes love to her, she cuts his head off.

Mick Jesus Christ.

Sally I'm only pretending. I won't do it really. Please don't stop. Don't stop!

Mick All right, I'm not stopping. What's she do with the head?

Sally She eats it.

Mick Why?

Sally Because he fucks better without a brain.

Mick I fuck better without a knife in my ear.

Sally *drops to the floor.*

Sally Look Mick, that's what she does.

Mick What about him?

Sally He dies.

Mick No kidding?

Sally And she eats the rest of him.

Mick I'll see you Thursday. (*He begins to pack up his knives.*)

Sally What's the matter?

Mick I think you're barmy, that's what's the matter.

Sally I was only pretending.

Mick But it's not . . . it's just not . . .

Sally What?

Mick Nice. It's not very nice.

Sally I think it's nice. I think it's fascinating. I gave you the book; I bet you didn't even read it.

Mick As a matter of fact I did.

Sally But you've never picked an animal for us.

Mick All right.

Sally What?

Mick There is an animal.

Sally What?

Mick Bedbug.

Sally In bed you mean. Boring.

Mick Please yourself.

Sally What do they do?

Mick This is stupid anyway.

Sally What do they do, Mick?

Mick Well, he turns her over on her back . . .

Sally Ha! Boring.

Mick Shut your face. Come here. He turns her over on to her back so she's helpless, right? He exposes her belly and he clambers on top of her. He makes his thing hard and it's sharp at the end, so he can drill a hole in her. He drills a hole for himself in her soft little belly.

Sally That's horrible.

Mick Animals are. They're uncivilised little bleeders. Why can't we act like normal human beings? Go to the pictures, go home, turn the telly on, fool around on the sofa. I want to be able to see your face.

Sally I don't like looking. I like how it feels but I don't like looking.

Mick Sally, making love is meant to be special.

Sally No it's not! It's not special! It's natural; it's what animals do. It's natural, but it's a secret. You mustn't tell anyone. It's a secret. Promise you won't tell anyone?

Mick Sally . . .

Sally (*to herself*) I promise.

Mick All I want in life . . .

Sally I promise!

Mick I want to be normal, that's all.

Scene Five

Somewhere in the zoo.

Anne *is mucking out or fixing up one of the enclosures.*
David *enters with a suitcase.*

Anne   That's it then is it? Hello goodbye.

David   Goodbye, yes.

Anne   Why is it that neither you nor your brother will
grow up and take some responsibility?

David   I don't know. You're the analyst.

Anne   I'm not an analyst, I was a therapist. A long
time ago.

David   Where's Alan?

Anne   He's at a Special General Meeting. Shareholders
and Animal Eaters.

David   He's very fond of you.

Anne   He's used to me. It's not the same. Do you
know why he came to see me all those years ago? He
came to see a psychotherapist because his father told
him to. No wonder the analysis was such a mess.

David   I thought the analysis was a mess because the
doctor fell in love with the patient.

Anne   Look, fuck Freud. I was a bloody good
therapist!

David   I'm sure you were.

Anne   I was. I was. I just couldn't stand all that
Oedipus stuff. What I wanted was a new language for it
all, not based on some Greek fairy tale, based in the real
world. The natural world.

David   Wasn't that about the time you met?

Anne   Yes. He wasn't in too bad a state when he came
to me. A bit confused, but passionate about animals.

We talked less and less about him and more and more
about animal behaviour. One afternoon we ran over
time and went to Regent's Park. Then on to dinner. We
got so close so quickly, before I knew what I'd done
we'd made love, promises, plans. Then I found myself
pregnant with Sally and rearing two puma cubs in the
bedroom. I found myself married.

David And happy?

Anne Oh, delirious. The zoo was fine, and I came up
with the Cob Deer Complex, the Starfish Syndrome,
the Tiger-fly. The tiger-fly eats its father, but its father
isn't a brutal insensitive mother-fucker, it's just a
hardworking little beetle. Innocent. And most fathers
are.

David Mine was just an exception.

Anne Granted. So was mine. Anyway, the language of
the natural world is infinitely more user-friendly than
Freud's scientific mumbo-jumbo, or Jung's hippy-
speak. I was poised to revolutionise the language of
psychotherapy.

David What happened?

Anne I had a nervous breakdown. I realised I'd done
the unforgivable. Freud appeared to me in a dream and
took away my breasts. I'd fallen in love with a patient.
You're a very good listener.

David Pardon?

Anne If you'd give me just two hours to get ready I'd
come with you, you know that, don't you? (*Pause.*) I
have made love to you in every place we've been.
Anywhere we've been alone, later I've made love to
you.

David I wish I had your imagination.

Enter **Alan.**

David Hello. Good meeting?

Alan You should have been there.

David I'm not a shareholder.

Alan I am. I used to hold twenty per cent. I'd worked out after the inheritance I should hold over eighty. Which I believe could be considered a healthy controlling interest. And means I could do anything. Anything I like. I could do anything I like. Anything.

David What are you going to do?

Anne Nothing.

Alan Nothing. Correct. Absolutely correct.

Anne Jesus.

David Why not? Alan, why not?

Alan Well, I can't, my old chum. Our accountants are Derby, Kay and Fletcher. Well, Derby, Kay or Fletcher cornered me just before we started and told me the old man has been selling off shares to unsuspecting old ladies for the last five years. He sold his controlling interest a month ago. Also, said Mr Derby, Kay or Fletcher, I ought to be aware that there was a strong move afoot of which I might not approve. It's all to do with the overheads, which we know are ridiculous, and the click click click of the turnstiles which we know is only intermittent, and the land value, which I had never realised is of course absolutely sky high.

David So what are you getting at?

Alan We've been sold out.

Anne What?

Alan Oh, we did vote. But seeing as we're now owned by some South African investment group it was a bit of a *fait accompli*. Sorry.

David Sorry for what?

Anne What do you think?

Alan We have to close the zoo.

Anne Jesus.

Alan Sorry.

Anne You bloody fool. You went in there completely unprepared!

Alan I had no idea.

Anne What are we going to do?

Alan I have no idea.

David What about the animals?

Anne This is your entire life, and you just let them . . .

Alan I did my best! What do I do about that Anne? Tell me. What do you do when your very best simply isn't good enough?

David What about the animals?

Alan *leaves abruptly.* **Anne** *glowers at* **David**.

David Look, it's nothing to do with me.

She leaves, livid. **David** *shouts after her.*

Look, I'm no use here! I've got to go somewhere I'm some use!

David *is left alone for a few moments. He picks up his case as* **Sally** *enters as a penguin.*

Sally Where are you going?

David Paradise.

Sally Can I come?

David You too?

Sally Mummy's in love with you, isn't she? I can't see it myself, but looking at Daddy I'm not surprised. She hates Daddy. They both hate me.

David What's the matter with you all?

Sally We're related.

David You're bloody English, that's the problem.

Sally Did you love your mother? I don't think there's any such thing as love. I think someone made it up to make people do things they don't want to. Love's got nothing to do with being friendly or decent. It's got nothing to do with liking each other. And it's certainly got nothing to do with fucking.

David I beg your pardon?

Sally I knew you'd be shocked. I bet you have the most beautiful dreams. I bet you don't dream of women, I bet you dream of animals. Enjoy yourself in Paradise.

The lights fade. The sounds of animals fade and the space slowly fills with the sound of dozens and dozens of people.

Act Two

Mauritius

Scene One

Port Louis. **David**'s *ship has just docked. He emerges with luggage like a man who has travelled half the world and no one remembered to wake him.*

All around him are the sounds of people shouting in English, French, Hindi, Chinese and patois. A hot, busy babble.

A young Hindu runs up and takes **David**'s *luggage from the space he just found for it, and stands there grinning.*

David No thank you, I'm waiting for someone. No, thank you very much. No thanks. No. I'm waiting for someone.

Nirad You must realise that if I put your bags down someone far less reliable will pick them up straight away.

David You speak English.

Nirad No. I speak Hindi. English I know a little, and French, and a little Chinese, but I speak Hindi. This pleases my father but it is by my own choice.

A young Chinese woman appears.

Lei Mr Ramsay! Mr Ramsay?

David Me! Yes. Ramsay.

Nirad Lei!

Lei Mr Ramsay?

David Yes.

Lei My name is Lei Chu Tang. My father is a good friend of Sir Michael Palmer, who has been unavoidably detained.

Nirad Sir Michael's daughter disappeared the night before last, although this is no concern of ours.

Lei He is asking my father's advice. My father will say 'Forget her'.

Nirad In fact it is common knowledge that Sir Michael's daughter has run off with a German seaman, a practice which seems to be becoming more and more acceptable here.

A young Creole is passing with a large sack of grain. His name is **Victor**.

Lei I must first of all say how honoured I am to be the first to greet the much talked-about 'Birdman'. I have been told of your great reputation by Sir Michael, who has instructed me to say: 'Welcome Birdman!'

Victor *is struck by the phrase. He observes them in silence.*

Nirad You are very small for an Englishman.

David I'm Welsh.

Nirad I'm Hindu.

Lei You're Mauritian. We are an integrated society, Mr Ramsay.

Nirad As my father would no doubt explain to you, that over his dead body, we are an integrated society.

Lei This is Nirad, Mr Ramsay. He is my very special friend in spite of all the sociological and ideological barriers between us.

Nirad And even in spite of my father.

Lei We are a modern equivalent of your Romeo and Juliet or as translated into West Side New York to become relevant to the sixties, we are Tony and Maria of the eighties here in the multi-racial community of Mauritius.

Nirad (*sings*) 'Everything's free in America, OK by me in America . . .!'

Lei I teach him. My current paper is on 'Popular American Culture and its Relationship to Economic Imperialism'.

David Very nice.

Nirad (*sings*) 'I gotta feeling there's a miracle due, gonna come true, coming to me . . .!' Taxi!

Scene Two

The back of a taxi. **Nirad, Lei** *and* **David** *are travelling along a bumpy road, crammed in with luggage.*

Nirad Mauritius is a small but densely populated island. Here the French, English, Creoles, Muslims, Hindus and Chinese live together in peace and harmony. On your left is Government House, and the statue of our own dear Queen Victoria, long live the Queen even though she's dead.

Lei Nirad is regarded as one of the most enthusiastic tour guides on the island.

Nirad And very cheap.

Lei But he got dismissed for making up his own facts.

Nirad That Lei makes up for me.

Lei All of which are true. Give examples.

Nirad Mauritius is chronically over-populated. There are one thousand people per square mile. Thirty per cent of them are unemployed. Half of them are under twenty-one. There is much hardship, much political unrest, and an atmosphere of tension, mistrust and violence.

Lei Marxism Today.

David I'm not a sociologist.

Nirad The oldest inhabitants are the French and British colonialists who introduced the Africans by importing them as slave labour. When Creole slaves refused to work any longer in the cane fields or were not fit to, the British turned to India for a new energetic labour force. The Indians who came were free men but earned only their food, and died at an average age of thirty-four. Fifty years later they formed a small union, and all lost their jobs. The British turned to China for yet another eminently exploitable labour force.

David Was he sacked for content or presentation?

Nirad But having got us here, now they leave us entirely alone. On your right is HMS *Mauritius*, which is definitely not a British garrison because the British Army is definitely no longer here. The soldiers are used only for internal security.

Lei Beating up Hindu trade unionists.

Nirad My friend is political.

Lei My second paper was on the politics of suppression worldwide.

Nirad The Mauritians export each year a crop of sugar worth tens of millions of pounds but the people remain poor enough to accept food aid from India.

David A lot of people must have died at this crossroads.

Lei Why?

David It's where the tourists finally throw themselves

out of the taxi. I'm not a political person, I'm sorry. I'm here because of the animals.

Nirad The natural history of Mauritius is of course a very intriguing one . . .

David I know. How many papers have you done?

Lei Thirty-two. Education is of absolute importance.

David It's all facts though, isn't it? I can never get excited by facts.

Nirad The following facts may be of some interest . . .

The taxi sounds its horn. Blackout.

Scene Three

A large room in a now unused wing of a large colonial house. There are french windows, in one corner a camp bed and, in another, a marble bust of an old colonial Englishman.

David *is asleep in the bed.*

Victor *appears in the window, holding in his hand a bird with its throat cut. He creeps carefully in and places the bird at the foot of the camp bed, on top of* **David**'s *feet.*

David *wakes up and screams his head off.* **Victor** *remains calm until he has finished, then quite calmly leaves.*

David *discovers the bird, first with distaste and then with pity.*

Enter **Palmer** *in a dressing-gown.*

Palmer A dream of murder?

David *shows him the bird.*

Palmer Ahah. Voodoo.

David It's a Pink Pigeon.

Palmer Good. Birds are good, generally speaking, and mammals are bad.

David I've come three thousand miles to save the Pink Pigeon and I'm greeted with this.

Palmer Heavy on irony, voodoo. Oh, my name's Palmer. Sir Michael. Call me Michael. No, call me Mike.

David Hello. This is your . . .

Palmer Home. I suppose so. (**Palmer** *smiles and sits.*) Are you comfortable here? There's no furniture in this wing any more.

David I'm very grateful. I was expecting to work from a damp Andrassi. What happened to the furniture?

Palmer Oh, a little Muslim village a few miles away didn't make it through the typhoons this year. I said they could choose what they wanted. They chose everything. Except the graven image there.

David That's very philanthropic of you.

Palmer Oh, I own nothing here. It all belongs to the corporation. So do the villagers. So do I.

David Would you like to see a bird?

Palmer Yes I would, I'd like that very much.

David *goes to a wooden cage and takes out a Pink Pigeon.*

David They're one of the rarest. I brought this one from Jersey. It's one of the last in captivity.

Palmer She's beautiful.

David She's a beauty. We won't be able to keep those cocks off you will we?

Have you always been interested in this?

Palmer Dear me no. I just heard you needed somewhere, and as the villagers had cleared the decks, it seemed the perfect thing to do. I believe it's called going with the flow. Do you go with the flow?

David Only so far as it helps me pick up enough momentum to bang my head against the next brick wall.

Palmer I've stopped doing that. I'm getting very good at it. There's another riot brewing at the refinery so I took decisive action yesterday and cycled home. I got home to find my daughter had run off, so with great presence of mind I made a lemon mousse.

David I was sorry to hear about your daughter.

Palmer She's gone. I like lemon mousse more than I like fuss so I didn't make a fuss, I made a lemon mousse instead. Of course, my wife doesn't understand me at all.

David I'm not sure I do entirely.

Palmer You know this island is full of the most wonderful people; fascinating people I'd never even spoken to. Until one day last month. I ran out of tobacco in town and went into a shop there. There was an old Chinaman in the corner, Lei's father, and he made absolutely no move to serve me. There I was, one of the wealthiest men on the island in the shop of one of the poorest and instead of falling over himself to please me he just sat there smiling, while I became irritable, then annoyed, and finally downright rude. I demanded service. So he offered me a carrot.

David I don't understand.

Palmer That's the point. You see, you ask for tobacco and you get a carrot. You throw the carrot at the shopkeeper and you get an inscrutable smile. You ask 'Why are you smiling?' And he hits you on the head with a bamboo stick. You get angry, you threaten him, insult him . . . he smiles. Then he lights a cigarette, and offers you a drag. His way of starting a conversation.

David Was it a good conversation?

Palmer Yes it was. Why a carrot? Why not? Why a cigarette? Why not? Why that smile? I was in that shop for three days. Talking to the kindest, wisest man I'd ever met.

David What kept you there?

Palmer That smile, and the truth he spoke. There are four holy truths and an Eightfold Path that leads from a small grocer's shop in Port Louis to a state of being . . . well, so far I've only glimpsed it. Sun'll be up soon . . . (*He stands and looks out.*) Today, well spent/Will make all yesterdays a dream of happiness/And all tomorrows an ectasy of hope. Thus is the salutation of the dawn. Sanskrit.

David Very nice.

Palmer Goodnight.

Palmer *leaves, returning briefly to hit* **David** *on the head with a rolled-up newspaper. There is a dull red light in the room now, and* **David** *holds a live bird in his hands.* **Palmer** *smiles and leaves him confused.*

Suddenly **Victor** *is there again. He enters the room carefully and takes the pigeon from* **David** *with great reverence, then smiles a broad smile and leaves him.*

David Well there's plenty more where that came from, after all; just help yourself! No! Don't let it . . . Oh God. (**David** *watches the bird fly away, then comes back from the window.*) Perhaps I'm in Cardiff. Perhaps I've been on the beer and it's all a dream.

Scene Four

The house.

David, Lei *and* **Nirad** *are working together carrying large empty cages into the room.*

Nirad Never believe the word of an Englishman.

David Not guilty.

Nirad He said he wished to help and here is the work, so where is Sir Michael?

David Meditating.

Lei You have to meditate for many years before you realise it's a complete waste of time.

David That's encouraging.

Lei No, that's enlightenment.

David I want to keep this area as clear as possible.

Nirad What's this?

David It's a humane trap. It doesn't hurt. (*He takes it off* **Nirad** *and it springs shut on his finger.*) Ahh! Bloody hell! Will you leave things alone.

Lei Have you been to Disneyland?

David I'm constantly reminding myself I'm not there now.

Lei I have to prepare for my special study group a report on 'Cultural Imperialism and the Infant with special reference to either Peanuts, ET or Walt Disney'. What do you think of Walt Disney?

David I think everything he drew looks and moves like a balloonful of blancmange.

Lei This is supposed to be for me a cultural exchange. You must answer my questions seriously or you are guilty of my exploitation.

David Sorry. I think Disney degraded every living species to a level below human, which is a remarkable achievement, OK?

Lei OK!

David *puts another large box on top of the one she is carrying.*

Nirad I have heard, and I should like to know if it is true, that although dead, Walt Disney is not buried but has been frozen and rests hidden in the Palace of the Ice Queen. In Disneyland.

Lei Cryogenics.

David Well, assuming that the idiot Disney was fool enough to get himself pumped full of liquid nitrogen, he probably is in a fairly well-preserved state. What he doesn't realise is that when they drain him off he'll fall from the bone like an overdone chicken. He's dead. And if there's any justice, instead of heaven or hell, God will have sent him straight to Fantasia.

Enter **Lady Palmer.**

Lady Palmer Mr Ramsay?

David Oh, call me David, please.

Lady Palmer I'm Lady Palmer. My husband mentioned to me over breakfast that you were entertaining a witch-doctor here last night.

David No, I've decided it was all a dream.

Lady Palmer My husband recently decided everything's a dream, but it cuts no ice with me. If he doesn't come to his senses I shall turn his life into a recurring nightmare. I am a Christian woman, Mr Ramsay, and don't find it the least bit difficult to tolerate all this disruption. However, I draw the line at black magic.

David Very sensible.

Lady Palmer It's a silly game that requires the slaughter of innocent creatures. Its perpetrators deserve the wrath of the Lamb. I hate this heathen island, Mr Ramsay. I believe it was created by God as a sort of religious zoo; a place we might observe all the half-baked idiotic ideologies of the world clamouring for attention and disappearing up their own belief systems. Eventually the Christian ethic will rise triumphant. What religion are you, boy?

Nirad Roman Catholic.

Lady Palmer There, you see.

Nirad If it pleases Krishna.

Lady Palmer And you?

Lei My mother is a Roman Catholic. But I wish to return to the old values of my people.

Lady Palmer Buddhist?

Lei Revolutionary Marxist.

Lady Palmer Typical. You must have a word with my husband. I'd rather he became a Revolutionary Marxist than a Buddhist. At least they don't smile at you all the time. And what about you?

David Me?

Lady Palmer Have you a religious b . . . b . . . b . . . belief?

David Well, I guess I believe in the miracle of creation and the order of the natural world, and of course in the principles of Gaia . . .

Lady Palmer Of who?

David Mother Earth?

Lady Palmer Oh dear me. That's all we were missing, a bloody pagan. Take my advice Mr Ramsay. Believe in our Lord and Saviour Jesus Christ or b . . .

b . . . b . . . believe in nothing. Good luck with your pigeons, Mr Ramsay. Please don't let them shit on the parquet. (*She leaves.*)

Nirad If I was to have a dinner party and could invite anyone I wanted I would invite all of my past lives.

Lei You would have to serve plenty of rotten meat.

Nirad Why?

Lei To feed all the worms.

They both laugh.

Lei (*to* **David**) Philosophical joke.

David I don't get it.

Nirad You see, Western and Eastern thought are completely incompatible.

Lei This is not true. The goal of Eastern thought is for thought to no longer exist. And in the West it has never existed anyway.

Nirad *laughs and exits.*

Lei That is another joke.

David Sorry.

Lei I am a very entertaining person.

David Yes you are.

Lei You think so?

David Yes.

Lei Then will you marry me?

David (*laughs*) Very good.

Lei No, that was not a joke. I am serious now; I wish to marry you. Not for sex and domestic slavery I hasten to add, but so that I can return with you to AMERICA!

David What?

Lei I could not get a scholarship. There are too many educated young people here now. They come back with all the words and make trouble, so scholarships are fewer now. So please, that I might return with you, I suggest marriage. Please consider this carefully.

She goes out. **Nirad** *runs back in.*

Nirad I've seen them from the window. The boys are coming.

David 100 rupees a bird, and not a penny if they've only one leg! I want them caught humanely.

He gives **Nirad** *some money. Before he can follow* **Nirad** *out,* **Lei** *returns.*

Lei Well, what is your answer?

David I think I need more time to think about it really. I mean, what about Nirad?

Lei If I wanted to marry Nirad I could never do so. My father has to give permission and my mother would never allow it.

David Why not?

Lei Because they are racist. The Chinese are appalling racists.

David Then they wouldn't let you marry me.

Lei Of course they would. You are an Englishman. If I marry you I could leave the island. If I could leave the island I could even marry Nirad, except I would already be married and Nirad could still not leave the island. Life is very complicated.

David What's your father like?

Lei Religious. He smiles. My sisters become stupid typists, he smiles. I wish to become educated, he smiles. My mother screams, he smiles. The world ends, he smiles.

David You never smile.

Lei If I smiled I would live in a house of grinning idiots. I wish to come to England where I will not have to become a stupid typist and where nobody ever smiles. So you marry me, yes?

David What about Nirad?

Lei Nirad loves me. Oh, I see. Good question.

Nirad *returns with a pink bird in a box.*

Nirad They have seven in all.

David Beautiful. How were they caught?

Nirad With the greatest consideration and gentleness. And at the greatest personal risk.

David Good. Bloody hell, it's sticky. Nirad we have a problem here. This isn't a Pink Pigeon. This is a dove that's been dipped in Ribena.

Nirad I see. So what do you suggest?

David I suggest you get my money back.

Nirad *exits and returns.*

Nirad They've gone.

David What a surprise.

Nirad On behalf of my boys I apologise. I shall let the birds go.

David No. I shall have to clean them off or they'll get stuck to everything. Find me some reliable boys, Nirad.

Lei I shall find you some reliable girls. (*She goes out.*)

Nirad I'm sure they did their best, but the pink birds are very hard to find. They are very rare you know.

He leaves to follow **Lei**. **David** *sits despondently.* **Victor** *appears in the doorway with a long thin bamboo cage, which he places down.*

David No! Don't open it. Is it alive whatever it is? Is it all in one piece?

The box is opened an inch or so. We hear the sound of pigeons.

David Oh, sweet Jesus. They're beautiful. Are they for me?

Victor *grins.* **Lady Palmer** *enters.*

Lady Palmer Mr Ramsay . . . I have just had a call from an old and dear friend of mine. An hour ago a group of young Hindus raided her aviary and stole six pure-bred white doves. I don't suppose you'd know anything about it?

David No, I . . . that's appalling, I . . .

Lady Palmer What's in here?

David Well, not doves obviously. Unless they'd been dipped in something . . . pink.

She turns to **Victor**.

Lady Palmer You're from the hills aren't you? Are you a convert?

Victor *smiles and undoes his shirt.*

A cross has been seared into his chest, leaving a vivid scar. **Lady Palmer** *winces.*

I despair, Mr Ramsay. I despair.

David Then you shall not go to heaven, Lady Palmer.

Scene Five

The house. A few weeks later. **David** *is tending his pigeons while* **Victor** *watches attentively.*

David The Pink Pigeon is the perfect example of natural selection at its worst. The real problem with

breeding them is they don't bloody like one another.
Thanks to you we've now got six potential breeding
couples; thirty-six possible combinations and no two of
them can bear to stand on the same bloody branch, let
alone fornicate. And look at that. Call that a nest? Call
that a nest, you miserable bloody thing? And there's not
one of them learnt that the only kind of egg you lay
from a perch twelve feet above the ground is a
scrambled one! They're the stupidest bloody species
I've ever come across. As for this one, look at him. He's
a pedigree bloody pigeon him, look. Pink as you like,
but he's only tried to mate once in three weeks; and that
was with his water dish. Come on boyo, make an effort.
It's the survival of your species we're talking about.
They think I'm mad. Who does he think he is, they say.
We don't want to fuck. We don't like it. My mum and
dad were decent, they never fucked, so why should I?
They think I'm mad. I think I'm mad. Sometimes I
wish you spoke English.

Victor I do.

David *looks up in amazement.*

David Well for six bloody weeks you haven't.

Victor *smiles.*

Is that it? Is that your entire contribution? Why haven't
you said anything up until now? Christ, I've probably
told you my entire life story.

Victor Birds. Birds. More birds. And your mother.

David I don't believe this.

Victor She taught you how to mend a wing with
matchsticks, and never stopped reminding you that you
should have married when you had the chance.

Enter **Lei** *and* **Nirad** *carrying a large package.*

Nirad We have it.

David Careful what you say, I'm being bugged.

Lei Married who?

David What?

Lei Nothing.

Nirad It was sent to the Corporation. Everything is sent to the Corporation.

David Of all things to go missing; the one thing I brought from England with trepidation. I almost didn't.

Nirad Why not?

David Superstition I suppose.

Nirad Then why?

David Because I'm not superstitious. Besides it's good barter. The museum here only has a skeleton. I'm not sure how genuine this is, but it might buy me some museum facilities. Please God, some more facilities. The Curators'll love this. It's about the same age they are.

As the final wrapping comes off the stuffed dodo **Victor** *leaps back.*

It's all right. It's not real. It's all wire and turkey feathers.

Victor *circles the dodo then goes up to* **David.**

Victor When the time comes I shall take you to my fathers. I will not seek their consent for they are old and would refuse. But once it is done they will welcome you.

David Er, good.

Victor Or they will be displeased, and we shall die together.

David I can't wait.

Victor *leaves.*

What was that all about?

Nirad Superstition. If you ask me all Creoles are
extremely pretentious about these things.

David What are you doing here anyway? I thought
you had a job of work to do?

Nirad Thirty-two per cent of the adult male
population of Mauritius is unemployed . . .

David You told me that.

Nirad And the other sixty-eight per cent are on strike.
General strike. We are very good at them. Strikes are
good things. They make poor men richer, that's all yes?

David Yes.

Nirad Then why the fuss?

Enter **Palmer**, *still in pyjamas.*

Palmer Ah, Nirad. Have the Hindu people any laws
to prevent an Englishman declaring himself a Hindu?

Nirad Mike, you may declare this if you wish. No
Hindu will take a blind bit of notice.

Palmer So theoretically I am able to become a Hindu?

Nirad Could you bow to a flower?

Palmer I could possibly nod.

Nirad Then you could possibly become a Hindu.

Palmer (*to* **Lei**) What about the Buddha? Is it
possible I might come close to the Buddha?

Lei It is impossible to be far away from the Buddha. If
you hate the Buddha with all your heart, then you are
still with the Buddha.

Palmer What if I were someone who had never heard
of the Buddha?

Lei You probably are the Buddha.

He goes, deep in Western thought.

David Do you think he's all right?

Nirad Yes. But he must have transgressed severely in his previous life.

David How do you know?

Nirad He was born a Christian in Middlesex.

Palmer *returns.*

Palmer I almost forgot. A worldly matter. The labourers on the Allied Estates are demanding eight per cent. Should I give it to them?

Nirad Give them ten?

Palmer All right.

Nirad On the other hand, fifteen would be very acceptable.

Palmer Whatever. How are the birds?

David More interested in the afterlife than this one.

Palmer Very wise.

David Very, very stupid.

Palmer I really must get dressed soon.

Palmer *leaves.* **Nirad** *follows. Left alone,* **Lei** *glares silently at* **David.**

David I'm still thinking about it!

She snaps her book shut in a temper and flounces out.
David *moves the dodo in front of the pigeons' cage.*

You see that? It's dead. Let that be a lesson to you. Don't give me that vacuous look . . . oh, you darling. You beautiful child, well done. It's lovely. (*He carefully removes a pigeon's egg from the cage and shows it to the male.*) And if you haven't fertilised that, I'm going to sell you to Dulux.

Enter **Lady Palmer.**

Lady Palmer Stealing eggs, a boy of your age?

David Bet your life. If I leave it in the cage they're more likely to play rugby union with it than sit on it. (*He places the egg on a towel in a hat, and holds it close to him.*)

Lady Palmer I'm hardly qualified to tell, but I don't think my husband's very well. What do you think?

David I think he's fine.

Lady Palmer You see, when one has been forced to spend one's life in an environment that is not at all like the home one remembers, one either finds some faith to hang firmly on to or one goes quite mad.

David Which did you choose? Sorry.

Lady Palmer I'd like you to leave.

David It was a stupid joke.

Lady Palmer Not the joke. The b . . . b . . . b . . . birds. I'd like you to pack all this up and leave my house. Please, as soon as possible.

David You can't be serious.

Lady Palmer I don't want them here. This is my house.

David But if I disturb this lot now they'll never breed . . . I might as well just set them free.

Lady Palmer I'm sure they'd appreciate that.

David What the hell do you know about it?

Lady Palmer I've had enough. Living in this hell on earth is bad enough without having them in the house.

David Who?

Lady Palmer These p . . . p . . . p . . . people!

David I see.

Lady Palmer No, I'm not a racist Mr Ramsay, but I need this house. I need it empty and silent. Free of human sweat and hope and chatter. And safe. My husband and I are too old for alternatives.

David He seems very happy.

Lady Palmer He chants to himself and goes around dinging a little bell. I don't call that happy, I call that mentally disturbed. He's a middle-aged English aristocrat; he has no business being happy. Now I want you, and these b . . . b . . . birds, and the rest of them. . .

David No! No! You leave me and my birds out of it! It's started now, after six weeks' work, and I'm not going to let you destroy it all on some racist whim! God, anywhere you go the English are always the same!

You're like the rest of your bloody country; self-centred, myopic and bloody soulless! And in your case, mad. It's not your husband, it's you. You're completely bloody insane. Clinically probably, but certainly insane. (*He takes the egg out of the hat and sits with it.*)

Lady Palmer I am not insane. I am Church of England. Did you know, when they first began to use electrocution to slaughter pigs, the owner of the abattoir noticed that the few pigs that failed to die showed a marked alteration in behaviour. Instead of squealing little horrors, they became calm, contented piglets. And from that they developed ECT. I've been to the slaughterhouse in my time. Seven times, but never again.

David I'm sorry.

Lady Palmer It was another patient that told me the medical staff were often impressed by religious conversion; sometimes even concluding the treatment. So after my seventh electrocution I saw the light. Hallelujah!

David Can I ask why you were there in the first place?

Lady Palmer Have you ever lived in England?

David No.

Lady Palmer There are things we tend not to talk about.

David I'm sorry.

Lady Palmer One's father raping one's daughter for instance. We keep that sort of thing so quiet if ever we do mention it, it tends to be whilst screaming. Stay if you wish.

David Thank you. Cheep cheep cheep. Cheep cheep cheep. Cheep cheep cheep.

Lady Palmer What are you doing?

David I'm pretending I'm its mother.

Scene Six

The house. Late night.

David, Lei, Nirad *and* **Palmer**, *still in pyjamas, are sitting up late.*

David *and* **Nirad** *are drunk,* **Palmer** *is sitting cross-legged.* **David** *finishes singing a gentle hymn in Welsh. They all applaud.*

Palmer Bravo.

Lei Very good.

David I'm drunk.

Lei Now Nirad's turn.

Nirad I have nothing I can do.

David I haven't been drunk since she died.

Palmer What about the egg?

Lei *uncovers it and they all look.*

Lei Cheep cheep cheep.

David This is ridiculous. It's not going to hatch for ages. Go to bed, all of you.

Palmer If you stay awake for the egg then we stay awake for the egg.

Lei Nirad, stay awake. Do your party piece.

Nirad I haven't got one.

Palmer I had one once, I think.

David Well somebody think of something before I fall asleep.

Lei I could read you another paper.

David No! Do that and we'll all drop off.

Palmer Nirad! Party piece!

Nirad All right. There is something. My father's father came here from the Tamil region. Tamils are the holiest and purest of the Hindu people. We can attain such purity of the spirit that it becomes possible to walk on fire, or to pierce our skin and feel no pain. (*He takes out a long, skewer-like needle.*) Today is a holy day.

David What's that?

Lei Nirad, you wouldn't. Please don't let him. He will make an awful mess.

David I'd rather you didn't; I'm a vegetarian.

Nirad It is a test of my fitness for life. (*He stands and raises the needle to his cheek.*)

Lei No.

David Tell me when he's finished.

Nirad *presses the needle into his cheek. He pushes it as far as it will go, but it will not pierce. He pulls it back a couple of inches and stabs towards his cheek.*

Nirad Ow!

David What happened?

Nirad I hurt myself.

Lei Serves you right.

Nirad I am impure. I have eaten meat.

Lei Nirad, your whole family do.

Nirad My family is in disgrace. I have drunk alcohol.

David Look, calm down and have another Guinness.

Nirad The Westerner has made us wretched.

Lei You watch too many of those awful Indian movies.

Palmer Nirad, the needle can never represent your freedom or whatever. The needle is part of your people's past. Throw it away. The present is your freedom, and it's our freedom, everyone's freedom, because the present is where we are. And we're together here.

Nirad Don't give me all that Buddhist bullshit!

Lei Shh.

David What?

Lei I heard something.

Palmer The egg.

David Not yet, it can't be.

They uncover the egg and look closely.

Palmer Cheep cheep cheep.

David Cheep cheep cheep. Come on.

Lei Cheep cheep cheep. Nirad.

Nirad Cheep cheep cheep.

Lady Palmer *enters in a dressing gown to find them in a circle cheeping.*

Lady Palmer I came down to complain about your waking me. Now I'm not sure you have.

Palmer We're keeping an all-night vigil for the hatching of the egg. Can you remember, do I have a party piece?

Lady Palmer If you've forgotten it I'm only too relieved. What are you doing?

Lei We are listening for the chick to tap on the side.

Lady Palmer *joins the silent circle.*

Lady Palmer Well I suppose this is faintly more interesting than yet another Dick Francis.

David No . . . nothing.

They all relax. **Nirad** *turns to the bust.*

Nirad Who is this?

Palmer I've no idea. He was here when we arrived.

Nirad It's not your father?

Palmer No. It's someone's father, I've no doubt.

Nirad I think he's very ugly. I would prefer to see him smashed to pieces.

Palmer Be my guest.

Lady Palmer What?

Palmer I've abandoned possessions.

Lady Palmer I haven't.

Palmer I don't own him. In fact quite the reverse. I hereby abandon all possessions I never truly owned.

Nirad Does that include my people?

Lady Palmer Are you drunk?

Nirad No, I am oppressed. I am an oppressed person, aren't I Lei?

Pause. Everyone ignores him.

I sometimes wish that I could learn the trick of the English. I wish I could learn to feel nothing. (*He pierces his tongue with the long needle. It seems not to hurt.*)

Lei Nirad? Nirad!! Oh Nirad.

David Bloody hell.

Lady Palmer You bloody little heathen nutcase.

Lei No. I think it is a political gesture.

David Who by? Sado-Masochists Against Racism?

Palmer Are you in pain?

Nirad *shakes his head.*

Lady Palmer Liar.

Nirad (*incoherent for obvious reasons*) It's not a political gesture, it's a personal one.

David That's the trouble with extreme political gestures. It's hard to understand exactly what you're getting at.

Palmer Is there any pain?

Lei How are you going to get it out?

Nirad Are you going with David?

Lei Shall I put it out?

Nirad Are you going with him?

Lei Sir Michael, would you help me please?

Palmer If you're ready Nirad, I'd like to help take the needle out.

Nirad *nods. They try to pull the needle and he screams.*

Lei More gently.

Palmer I'm being as gentle as I can.

Lady Palmer Pull it out in one go, like an elastoplast.

They try again. **Nirad** *screams and squirms.*

Palmer Perhaps we should just . . .

Lei No, we must help him.

Lady Palmer Help them.

David I'm a conscientious objector.

Palmer I think he's in a lot of pain now.

David All right. (*He puts down the egg and the hat in front of the bust.*) I think you're probably right about one swift pull, but in one movement, right?

Palmer I'm no expert. Would you?

David Oh God, all right. I suppose he's only got himself to blame.

David *pulls the needle out.* **Nirad** *screams, spitting blood.*

Nirad Aaargh! American son of a bitch!

Lei It's all right, Nirad; the needle has gone.

Nirad The needle has not gone! (*He snatches it back.*) I love you! You get married to this son of a bitch! You leave Mauritius, you leave me! I hate you! I hate Americans! I hate this stupid American birdcrazy mother fucker!

Nirad *threatens* **David** *with the needle. Everyone shouts.*
David *steps back onto the hat and egg. Things calm down,*
Lei *comforting* **Nirad.**

Lei Nirad, I love you. It's you I love. I love you.

David *discovers the broken egg.*

David It's broken.

Palmer Forget it. It's past. Leave the past; return to
the present.

David But it's broken.

Palmer No past; no regret, no pain. Return to the
present.

David But it's still broken.

Palmer No! Well, I mean . . . yes, but . . . um . . .

Nirad I am sorry.

Lei He is sorry.

David I knew it was there. You know how time slows
down. There was the needle. The needle could hurt me.
But I could step back. But there was the egg. I knew it
was there. But back I stepped, and here I am. And here
it is. (*He dips his finger in the egg.*) So what happens
now?

Suddenly **Victor** *appears, dressed in an elaborate costume
of turkey feathers and other parts of birds. He goes
straight to* **David.**

Victor You come now.

*The noise of birds and drums. The lights dim and the stage
clears.* **David** *and* **Victor** *cross it, going deep into the
forest and high.* **David** *is half unwilling but* **Victor** *is
adamant. Bird-like creatures enter if possible. They are
men of* **Victor**'s *village.* **David** *enters among them.*

Suddenly he is thrown into a pool of light. It is dim all around him. He stands up and peers into the darkness. Strange noises surround him. He is terrified.

When he sees what is in the pit into which he has been thrown, he begins to make a sound himself, half scream, half astonishment.

Act Three

England

Scene One

The zoo surgery.

Alan *enters and puts on a white coat. It has a single blood stain just below the right breast. He takes out a tape recorder and loops the microphone around his neck, turns it on and tests it.*

Alan Good morning Bea. It's Monday the fifth and it's ten-fifteen. (*He takes a box of syringes and a box of capsules to the operating table. He goes out briefly and returns with a box of mice.*) Mice. Common or garden, I can't remember the Latin and someone tore the label off years ago. Mousus minimus. (*He injects three mice.*) I'm using the hydrocyanic at a ten per cent solution for anything smaller than a rabbit, unless it's a reptile; tell Robin that, will you. There are four specimens. (*He looks in the box but the last has disappeared.*) Three specimens. I'm sorry, I know how you feel about mice. Just be thankful we found the alligator. Ha ha. Oh, by the way don't type this but we're running out of this stuff again; could you place another order? Er . . . ten, twenty. They're dead. (*He puts the mice aside and checks his list.*) Guinea pigs. Wouldn't anyone take six fucking guinea pigs?

*Enter **Mick**, with his Adidas bag and carrying slaughterhouse gear.*

Mick Something smells in here.

Alan Iodine, ether . . .?

Mick Not clean. Something shat or something, smell it?

Alan Where have you come from?

Mick Mammal house.

Alan It's on your shoe.

Mick Shit.

Alan Who are you?

Mick I'm the YOP.

Alan We're closed.

Mick Well I'm at Spiller's actually. They said we've got a contract here.

Alan The larger mammals, and the whale I think. You're a bit early; we're still on the children's corner. Would you like to come back later; I don't think butchering gerbils would be economically viable, do you?

Mick Don't ask me, it's your zoo. I'm just on contract. Tell you the truth I can't stand slaughterhouse work. Who wants to work in a slaughterhouse all their life? I was meant to go to Dewhurst's. I wanted to be a family butcher. I mean there's not much skill in the killing; it's all electric. Mind you, this would be a challenge. There's some big bastards here. Wouldn't it be quicker just to break their necks?

Alan This way's humane.

Mick Wouldn't it be more humane? I'd rather have me neck broken, definitely.

Alan Shut up.

Mick I know your daughter.

Alan Yes?

Mick School together. What'll you do with the giraffe and that?

Alan Use a bigger needle.

Mick Need a hand?

Alan Certainly not. Look, if you want to be useful there are some . . . well some of our debris won't go whole through the door of the incinerator.

Mick It'll cost you. I ain't doing no favours on twenty-five quid a week.

Alan I'll pay. Let me show you.

Mick No need. I'll follow my nose. (**Mick** *goes to the door*.) How is Sally?

Alan Why?

Mick I haven't seen her for a bit. She's great. Bit unusual, you know. No offence. But she ain't normal.

Mick *goes.* **Alan** *turns back to his work, a little shaken.*

Alan All right, Bea. Guinea pigs, four specimens, dead. (*He looks at his clipboard and laughs.*) Would you believe lemmings next?

Anne *enters in evening dress.*

Anne No I didn't.

Alan What?

Anne Spend the night with him. As if you'd care. I spent the night in a motorway lay-by because we have a leak in the petrol tank. It was an awful dinner, I had my knee groped and breasts fondled, but the good news is Windsor will take the rhino! And Chessington are going to let us know about the wolves. It's a good possibility.

Alan Good.

Anne Good? It's bloody marvellous. I had to act like a Soho hostess, I'm bloody freezing, and all you can say is 'good'. I'm tired and cold, hold me.

Alan I am a bit busy at the moment.

Anne Alan, leave that alone for a minute. Leave it alone and come here.

Alan Why?

Anne (*as if to a child*) Come here.

Alan *goes part way to her.*

Anne Now kiss me.

Alan It's half past ten in the morning, don't be absurd.

Anne Don't you dare call me absurd! I have spent too much emotional energy on you to be ignored for the next twenty years! Touch me. Just touch me. (*She gets close to him.*) Touch me. (*Pause.*) Touch me. (*Pause.*) Touch me. (*Pause.*) Please. (*Pause.*) Touch me.

She touches him, he pulls away slightly. She touches him again, which distresses him more. She ends up beating him. He just raises one arm to defend himself and she beats him until she is exhausted. Finally she is left hanging on to his arm, then she falls.

Alan Not this Anne, I really can't be bothered with this.

He leaves her. A telephone rings. **Alan** *ignores it,* **Anne** *pulls herself together and answers it.*

Anne Hello? Yes. Oh, that's wonderful. Thank you. (*Puts the phone down.*) Chessington will take the wolves.

Alan I may be finished by the weekend.

Anne Isn't that good news?

Alan I have to drain the aquarium. It seems the simplest way. (*He turns at the door.*) I did the wolves yesterday. (*He leaves.*)

Anne *looks for a cigarette but finds her packet empty. She* *looks in the pockets of* **Alan's** *lab coat and pulls out her hand suddenly with a small scream. On more careful inspection she brings out a small brown mouse, which sits on her hand sniffing around.*

Anne Hello. Careful. It's a long way down.

Scene Two

Sally *already onstage, huddled. Watches* **Mick** *with barrow.*

Mick Hi.

She continues to watch his work.

Mick I missed you.

Reaches out to touch her. She scuttles away.

Mick You want to play?

He tries to play, as with a kitten. She's reluctant.

Mick You want to eat?

He throws meat at her. She hisses at him.

Mick Sally, just give us a cuddle?

He approaches, she lashes out and scratches his face with four sharp wails.

Mick You stupid fucking bitch; it's just a job!

Sally You disgust me!

Mick Fuck me, it talks.

Sally You animal!

Mick I don't think so. What do you think happens out there in the real world? You think they all settle down for a nice long retirement? If no fucker ate them when they were young, and no fucker caught them when they were older, then some fucker is gonna come along and eat them when they're old. They ain't no one's best friend. Animals are meat for one another, that's all they are. Love animals? You might as well love hamburgers. Love is for us. We invented it for us.

Sally I hate humans.

Mick Then you're an animal.

She attacks him, scratching and biting, holding on.

Mick Shit, Sally. Sally. Shit.

Having forced him to curl up, she breaks away. Pins herself against a wall, lifts her chin and gives a scream, a howl, a chilling, echoing sound. Blackout.

Scene Three

The mammal house.

*Enter **Alan**, his white coat much bloodier. The elephant trumpets softly.*

Alan Here we are again then.

Anne *comes on in a hurry.*

Anne Alan! Alan! What on earth's going on?

Alan I'm nearly finished, that's what's going on. I'm tired and I shall get no rest until I've done all this. So let me do it in my own way which is swift now, and very efficient.

Anne I'm still trying to save some of these animals.

Alan What's the point? What's the point? (*He turns and busies himself.*)

Anne Darling, I think you should stop.

Alan Why?

Anne I think you've done enough.

Alan I'm fine.

Anne You're not.

Tell me how you feel. Can you do that for me? Try to name something inside that you feel.

Pause

Alan Clichés. Two thirds of the people are starving to death while we burn food by the ton. There are people losing limbs for the right to step out of the gutter and others losing their minds for the right to think. Twelve children die of hunger in the time it takes for me to eat a single mouthful. Most people in the world do nothing but suffer, and most of the rest do nothing. And I don't care. I don't care about them, not one of them. I don't care. My compassion and my pity and my caring is all for me. No one else. Oh, I've let you watch me wallow in it, my self-pity. I've splashed you with enough of it, and I've turned around and recognised the stain on you and in those moments I suppose I loved you, but that's all. I have never cared about you. Or them. I just . . . don't care. (*He pulls a bloody object from his pocket.*) This is the heart of a lion. (*He doesn't know what to do with it.*) That's interesting, isn't it?

Anne *goes to touch him.*

No.

She leaves him. He puts down the heart and wipes his hands. He turns to the elephant enclosure. She trumpets softly.

You had a reprieve didn't you, in all the excitement. It's over, I'm afraid. I don't think this'll hurt, but I have no idea really. I'm not sure. I hope it won't. It's this or shoot you and you'd hate the noise. (*He climbs into the enclosure.*) Or on the other hand you could just break my skull for me. No? I didn't think you would. Easy now. That leg there would have bothered you soon. It would have been a bad leg. It's a bit quiet

around here now isn't it? Let's find a nice wide vein in
this ear now, shall we? Time to die, you gentle, gentle
girl. (*He injects her.*) Steady. That's it. All over. Yes,
I did. I just did. Not because of him, no revenge.
Honestly, there's no revenge in this; this is just the
price of vegetables. I haven't the strength to put an end
to you for more than that. No hate, no blame. In fact,
thank you. For putting an end to him. Thank you.

She trumpets more softly. **Alan** *sits down and watches a
beetle scurry across the floor. He treads on it and twists his
foot. He takes out another hypo and phial, rolls up his
sleeve and injects himself. He rolls down his sleeve and
waits.* **Anne** *returns.*

Anne What are you doing in there?

Alan Just finishing off.

Anne Come out.

Alan In a while.

Anne Alan, I called a doctor. Alan?

Alan Yes? Who? Who'd you call?

Anne You don't know him. He's a good man.
Someone you can talk to.

Alan Uhhuh? I thought you were my therapist.

Anne We never finished. We can never finish now. I
fell in love with you. I love you. I can't do anything for
you now.

Alan Try me. Ask me questions. Let me talk.

Anne I'll always listen.

Alan Anne, Annie, ask me what happened in the
mammal house.

Anne What happened in the mammal house?

Alan My father . . . my father died.

Anne How do you feel about that?

Alan All right. Relieved.

Anne Guilty? Sorry. Leading you. I'm out of practice.

Alan That's all right. Anyway, the answer's no. Not guilty. Oh help. Ask me what happened in the mammal house.

Anne What happened in the mammal house?

Alan When?

Anne I don't know when. Alan, tell me what happened in the mammal house.

Alan No. I wasn't here.

Anne Do you want to tell me what happened?

Alan I don't know, I wasn't here. Except sometimes I remember I was so I must have been. Annie, Anne, ask me what happened here. Ask me what happened.

Anne Were you here?

Alan Yes. Yes I was.

Anne Tell me what happened.

Alan Sally was eight.

Anne Sally?

Alan Sally was playing. With her little zoo, the toy he bought her. She was eight. Sally was playing with her zoo in the mammal house; just beyond where you're standing.

Anne So what happened?

Alan I don't know, I'm not . . .

Anne What happened!

Alan The old man was playing too. He'd found young Sally playing with her zoo and decided he'd play too. It

must have been a Monday afternoon; there was no
public. He'd got down on his knees. Crawling around
playing zoos with his eight-year-old granddaughter.
Why not? After all, there was only an old elephant to
see.

Anne   See what?

Alan   I wasn't there.

Anne   Yes you were. See what?

Alan   Nothing. Playing.

Anne   What did you see?

Alan   I just saw the old man in a suit down on the
ground with Sally. That's all.

Anne   What did she see then, old Ellie the elephant
here; what did she see?

Pause

Alan   The old man on top of Sally, his chubby fingers
pulling at her knickers.

Anne   You saw that?

Alan   His hands around her waist, lifting her up so's
she had to sit on him. Sally and Grandad, face to face.

Anne   And what did you do?

Alan   Nothing.

Anne   Nothing? You did nothing. You just walked
away?

Alan   With Sally calling from the mammal house.

Anne   You shit. You cowardly little shit.

Alan   Ellie saw.

Anne   You saw too! You saw! You knew what he was.

Alan   He was my father.

Anne *leaves.* **Alan** *dies.*

Scene Four

The mammal house.

The sound of a huge door opening and closing. Sunlight spills across the floor for a moment, then is gone as we hear the door swing closed.

Sally *enters, normally for the first time. As she shouts, there is an echo.*

Sally You're all dead now! (*Pause.*) You're all dead now! (*Pause.*) You're all dead now! (*Pause.*) Now what?

The door opens again. **Sally** *hides in the shadows. The door closes and* **Mick** *enters carrying an old box. His footsteps echo as he looks around. Believing himself alone, he sets up the box in the centre and sits on it. Furtively he takes from his jacket a sketch pad and some charcoal. He begins to draw, hard straight lines, examining the empty enclosure in front of him.* **Sally** *reappears.*

Hello.

Mick *jumps and tries to hide his drawing.*

What are you doing?

Mick Nothing.

Sally What?

Mick Nothing.

Sally You were drawing. What were you drawing?

Mick Nothing.

Sally There are no animals now. Haven't been for months. What were you drawing?

Mick I wasn't drawing. I was sketching. It's called sketching.

Sally Sketching what?

Mick The bars. I was sketching the bars. I might do some paintings, of the enclosures. Empty cages.

She goes towards him, he backs off.

Look Sally, sorry . . .

She accepts this, but sadly. He moves off. She runs to him, turns him around, and kisses him, face to face. Then he smiles.

I'll see you.

He leaves. The door opens and closes off. **Sally** *turns and gasps. Someone is moving in the elephant enclosure.*

Sally Who are you? What are you doing here?

Victor *enters. He wears* **David**'s *suit. It doesn't quite fit.*

Victor Climbing out of this enclosure. Any objections?

Sally This place is closed to the public. It's closed to everyone, even me. You shouldn't be here.

Victor Well I am. I've got a question for you. What for were you doing all that yelling earlier?

Sally I can yell if I want. My mother says there's nothing wrong with yelling.

Victor Singing's better.

Sally I'm to yell as much as I like about whatever I like. There are no secrets.

Victor I have a secret.

Sally What?

Victor It's a secret. You're called Sally.

Sally How do you know?

Victor A little bird told me. That's a clue.

Sally That's Uncle David's.

Victor What?

Sally That suit you're wearing. It belongs to Uncle David. Where did you get it?

Victor I'm a friend of his.

Sally He's disappeared. He might be dead, we think. Look, what are you doing here?

Victor Waiting.

Sally What for?

Victor That's the secret. Almost time. (*He looks briefly at his watch and turns to leave the way he came.*)

Sally Can you get out that way?

Victor I know ways you never even dreamed of.

He goes. The doors open and close again. **Anne** *enters, looking for* **Sally**.

Anne You shouldn't be in here. We're not here to be morbid, we're here to get ourselves sorted out. Get our things together and go.

Sally *runs over and takes* **Anne**'s *arm. This is a nice surprise for* **Anne**. *They touch for the rest of the scene.*

Sally Where shall we go?

Anne Well . . . wherever you like.

Sally Paradise. You know, that island.

Anne Not that far, no.

Sally We could go and find Uncle David.

Anne Sally. (*Pause.* **Anne** *sits on* **Mick**'s *box.*) How do you feel?

Sally I don't feel anything much. I can remember things. I can remember mostly everything now, but I don't feel much. Except deep down, there's something. But it's very small.

Anne What's that? What do you feel deep down?

Sally Happy. Is that bad?

Anne No, that's wonderful. Come on let's get out of here.

The doors open and stay open. Light floods in. **Victor** *enters carrying a bale of straw. He turns and walks backwards to speak to* **Nirad** *and* **Lei,** *who follow carrying more straw and bundles of foreign-looking leaves.*

Victor Welcome to England! Gloomy and soulless but full of potential. (*To* **Anne** *and* **Sally**) Hello.

Lei Hello. Nirad.

Nirad Sorry. Hello.

Anne Hello.

Lei *and* **Nirad** *go for more supplies.*

Umm?

Victor My name's Victor.

Anne How do you do?

He laughs uproariously.

Victor I do all right. How do you do?

He laughs. **Sally** *laughs too.* **Anne** *smiles warily.* **David** *enters. When* **Anne** *sees him she gapes, then runs to him. He meets her and they embrace in silence. There is a pause, then* **Victor** *crosses to them and puts his arms around them both.*

Now this is what I call a how do you do. This is a better how do you do. (*To* **Sally**) Come and say how do you do.

He takes her arm and pulls her over. She joins them all in a ridiculous cuddle.

Anne Where have you been?

David On my way home for what seems like months. Hello Sally.

Sally Hello.

Victor *Moi aussi.*

Lei *and* **Nirad** *come in, put down their stuff, and watch.*

It's called a how do you do.

David Oh, these are my colleagues. This is Anne.

Anne Hello.

David This is Lei.

Lei Hello.

Lei *and* **Anne** *shake hands.*

Anne Hello.

David Nirad, Anne.

Nirad Hello.

Anne Hello.

They shake hands.

David And this is Victor Ngema.

Anne Hello.

Victor Hello.

David And this is Sally.

Sally Hello.

All Hello.

David Victor's my new partner. And Lei and Nirad are hoping for citizenship.

Nirad We have heard your country is going to the dogs, but it is not going to the dogs as fast as our country.

Lei Nirad has a lot to learn. We have come to England to experience true civilisation.

Anne Oh dear.

David Someone's got a lot to learn.

Lei I know I have.

David No, not you, as a matter of fact.

Mick *enters and looks at them.* **Anne** *gets embarrassed, and the group breaks up.*

Mick Pardon me. I don't know what you've got out here, but they're getting a bit jumpy.

Victor *leaves briskly.* **Lei** *and* **Nirad** *follow.* **Mick** *leaves with them curious.* **Sally** *follows.*

David Be careful. (*Pause.*) I'm sorry about this place. And about um . . .

Anne *shakes her head.*

Anne No, later. Not today. I'm too happy. I'll feel guilty later; for today I'm very happy to see you.

David Good. Er . . . me too. I mean it. I'm happy too. We've got something that might interest you. Special cargo. I thought there'd be plenty of space here.

Anne More than enough. The zoo's dead, David.

David Maybe we'll give it a new lease of life.

Anne I shouldn't think so.

David Wait and see.

The others return carrying a large wooden packing case, for animal shipping.

Anne What happened to you? We were told you'd completely disappeared. Then nothing.

David I was taken to a village so high up it wasn't even on the map. It's a small community descended from a bunch of slaves who thought fuck it and ran off. They live in almost total isolation; Victor was their city-man. Some of them hadn't seen a stranger in their entire history. He took both our lives into his own hands because of some prophecy of some sort. I was just in the right place at the right time.

Anne What do you mean?

David To be quite honest, I thought I was going to be sacrificed. I was scared shitless to be quite honest. I thought they were going to murder me in some gruesome ritual. I'd have run away but there was always a firm grip on my ankle or arm as they sponged me down and covered me in this perfumed mud. And there's him grinning all over his face, and they all started chanting. They chanted for bloody ages. Chanted for so bloody long I began to cry. That seemed to impress them. Now they were all grinning like lunatics. They led me off and formed a circle around a huge reed mat, but it wasn't a mat, it was a lid. They lifted up this gigantic lid, and there was the pit. I was scared out of my wits. They picked me up and threw me in it. I couldn't see a thing, except their faces up above smiling as if they thought they were doing me a favour. So I looked around. It was very dark. I couldn't make much out. Something was moving. I presumed it was there to eat me. Then someone lowered down a torch; the pit filled with that lovely flaming torchlight . . . and there was something there. In the middle of the light it stood, blinking its eyes and wondering why on earth it had been woken up at this ungodly hour. It was a dodo. And it looked at me, I swear to God, and it opened its beak and it made the daftest sound I've ever heard. And there were females roosting and younguns being sat on, and all around me these grinning bloody conservationists, showing off their handful of gods for the very first time.

Victor *opens the crate and* **Anne** *steps forward with*

David *to look,* **Sally** *and* **Mick** *join them. From the crate there issues an absurd cry which echoes around the mammal house.*

That's it. Sing, you bugger, sing!

The lights fade. **Palmer** *appears in a single spot. He still wears his pyjamas.*

Palmer (*smiling*)

And today, well spent,
Will make all yesterdays a dream of happiness
And all tomorrows an ecstasy of hope.
Thus is the salutation of the dawn.

Methuen Drama World Classics

include

Jean Anouilh (two volumes)
Brendan Behan
Aphra Behn
Bertolt Brecht (eight volumes)
Büchner
Bulgakov
Calderón
Čapek
Anton Chekhov
Noël Coward (eight volumes)
Feydeau (two volumes)
Eduardo De Filippo
Max Frisch
John Galsworthy
Gogol
Gorky (two volumes)
Harley Granville Barker
    (two volumes)
Victor Hugo
Henrik Ibsen (six volumes)
Jarry

Lorca (three volumes)
Marivaux
Mustapha Matura
David Mercer (two volumes)
Arthur Miller (six volumes)
Molière
Musset
Peter Nichols (two volumes)
Joe Orton
A. W. Pinero
Luigi Pirandello
Terence Rattigan
    (two volumes)
W. Somerset Maugham
    (two volumes)
August Strindberg
    (three volumes)
J. M. Synge
Ramón del Valle-Inclán
Frank Wedekind
Oscar Wilde

Methuen Drama Modern Plays

include work by

Edward Albee
Jean Anouilh
John Arden
Margaretta D'Arcy
Peter Barnes
Sebastian Barry
Brendan Behan
Dermot Bolger
Edward Bond
Bertolt Brecht
Howard Brenton
Anthony Burgess
Simon Burke
Jim Cartwright
Caryl Churchill
Complicite
Noël Coward
Lucinda Coxon
Sarah Daniels
Nick Darke
Nick Dear
Shelagh Delaney
David Edgar
David Eldridge
Dario Fo
Michael Frayn
John Godber
Paul Godfrey
David Greig
John Guare
Peter Handke
David Harrower
Jonathan Harvey
Iain Heggie
Declan Hughes
Terry Johnson
Sarah Kane
Charlotte Keatley
Barrie Keeffe

Howard Korder
Robert Lepage
Doug Lucie
Martin McDonagh
John McGrath
Terrence McNally
David Mamet
Patrick Marber
Arthur Miller
Mtwa, Ngema & Simon
Tom Murphy
Phyllis Nagy
Peter Nichols
Sean O'Brien
Joseph O'Connor
Joe Orton
Louise Page
Joe Penhall
Luigi Pirandello
Stephen Poliakoff
Franca Rame
Mark Ravenhill
Philip Ridley
Reginald Rose
Willy Russell
Jean-Paul Sartre
Sam Shepard
Wole Soyinka
Simon Stephens
Shelagh Stephenson
Peter Straughan
C. P. Taylor
Theatre Workshop
Sue Townsend
Judy Upton
Timberlake Wertenbaker
Roy Williams
Snoo Wilson
Victoria Wood

CPSIA information can be obtained
at www.ICGtesting.com
Printed in the USA
LVOW13s1019081216
516386LV00014B/409/P